Ian Markham is the holder of the Liverpool Chair of Theology and Public Life at Liverpool Hope University College.

D1126898

TRUTH AND THE REALITY OF GOD

TRUTH AND THE REALITY OF GOD

An Essay in Natural Theology

IAN MARKHAM

T&T CLARK
EDINBURGH

T&T CLARK LTD
59 GEORGE STREET
EDINBURGH EH2 2LQ
SCOTLAND

Copyright © T&T Clark Ltd, 1998

All rights reserved. No part of this publication may be reproduced,
stored in a retrieval system, or transmitted, in any form or by any means,
electronic, mechanical, photocopying, recording or otherwise,
without the prior permission of T&T Clark Ltd.

First published 1998

ISBN 0 567 08618 6

British Library Cataloguing-in-Publication Data
A catalogue record for this book is available from the British Library

BL
182
.M3450
1998

Typeset by Waverley Typesetters, Galashiels
Printed and bound in Great Britain by MPG Books, Bodmin

JESUIT - KRAUSS - McCORMICK - LIBRARY
1100 EAST 55th STREET
CHICAGO, ILLINOIS 60615

In memory of Beryl Evelyn Markham
(1927–1981)

Contents

Acknowledgements

This book has emerged through a long and complicated journey. Practically everyone who reviewed my *Plurality and Christian Ethics* (Cambridge: Cambridge University Press, 1994) thought that I needed to develop the argument which I sketch out in Chapter 8 – an argument from truth to God. This became the task of my Boundy Lectures at the University of Exeter. These lectures proved to be my last major public performance at that university. For the stimulation and friendship of the theological team there I am forever grateful. Since then, I have been enjoying conversations with colleagues at Liverpool Hope. For their support and interest in my work, I offer my thanks. To turn the lectures into a book, I was fortunate to be appointed the Frank Woods Fellow at Trinity College, Melbourne. This provided the much needed space to adjust the manuscript. Thanks are due to the following: Dr Evan Burge, for being a marvellous host; Dr Damian Powell and his wife Dieni for introducing me to Carlton's famous Lygon Street; Dr Scott Cowdell for long conversations on the state of theology in Australia (and other things); Michael Leighton-Jones for a delightful steak and (Oz) cabernet; Jodi and Richard Monfries for sharing my delight in Irish whiskey; John Adams for a trip to Aussie footie; Fr Colin Griffiths, SSM for his pride in Australian religion; Professor Allan Patience for understanding the path I am taking; and Fr Norman Curry for the day out in a national park; and finally Dr Chris Mostert for understanding how difficult a Saturday night can be when you are away from friends and family.

In the concluding stages a number of friends proved very helpful: Leslie Houlden and Shannon Ledbetter did me the kindness of checking the final manuscript. Whatever defects the book now has, it has fewer because of their help. In addition I am grateful to the publishers, who saw the manuscript through to a book, and for two excellent readers' reports both of which enhanced the book considerably.

My wife Lesley and my son Luke had to put up with my distracted moods as I sorted out the details of the argument. Finally, the book is dedicated to the memory of my mother. She gave me so much; but perhaps her infectious love of reading is the most significant contribution to this project. This dedication to my mother is made on behalf of all my brothers and sisters – Rosemary, Anthony, Jacqui, Debbie, and Michael; she was a great mum.

Introduction

Giving reasons for your faith is not in fashion. Fideism is in control. By fideism, I mean the decision to 'believe' is made on 'non-rational' factors. For some theologians it is a 'faith' decision, which is simply a response to the gospel. For others, it is more ecclesiological or philosophical; but for all such theologians, natural theology is not an option.

James Barr helpfully defined natural theology as follows:

> that 'by nature', that is, just by being human beings, men and women have a certain degree of knowledge of God and awareness of him, or at least a capacity for such an awareness; and this knowledge or awareness exists anterior to the special revelation of God made through Jesus Christ, through the Church, through the Bible.[1]

The foremost opponent of natural theology, as Barr discusses at some length, is Karl Barth. Some of the world's most able theologians are sympathetic to Barth's work: it is felt by many that Barth's contribution survives in our postmodern world, because he spotted the problem of metaphysical knowledge and offered a robust response which is immune from secular critique. The Barthian argument runs thus: all speculation separate from revelation will end up being pure guesswork. Puny, sinful, human minds cannot get to know the divine, holy, transcendent. Therefore natural theology is always doomed to failure. For the Barthian, the choice is always between agnosticism or revelation. Apart from Christ, there is no knowledge. It is in trusting the Word, which is Christ,

1

that we can have knowledge of God. The primary locus for
encountering the Word is in the preaching of the word, which
takes place within the community of the Church.

Despite the brilliance and neatness of the Barthian position,
I find it disquieting. The difficulty is obvious: revelations
abound in this world, how do I know the Christian one is the
true one? This is the unanswered question. The Barthian is
only able to repeat that it is a matter of faith: a matter of
trusting the Christian community that gives us Christ.

Those who are more explicitly postmodern and historicist
are developing more sophisticated 'reasons' for rejecting
natural theology. Of these theologians, John Milbank is the
best example. He is an advocate of 'radical orthodoxy'. For
Milbank, rationality is internal to a tradition. There is no such
thing as 'traditionless reasons'. If there are no reasons
transcending traditions, then, of course, it becomes impossible
to have an external reason for joining a particular tradition.
Traditions justify themselves, using their own criteria. To
search for reasons that are external to that tradition is considered to be philosophically naive. So for Milbank conver-
sions to the Christian tradition are explained theologically.
In practice his explanation looks 'sociological'; people become
Christians because they meet lots of Christians. Once again,
fideism is the answer.

Even the liberals, at the opposite end of the spectrum, on
this issue end up at the same destination. Schleiermacher
was the father of this tradition. Experience lies at the heart of
his theology. Modern day disciples share this emphasis. So
George Newlands makes the awareness of the presence of
God central to his theology.[2] Meanwhile Gareth Jones has at
the heart of his theology a mystery which involves 'the spiritual
primacy of immanence'.[3] Both Newlands and Jones believe
that natural theology is part of the unobtainable premodern;
if it survives at all, it only does so in an attenuated form. In
the end, Kant and Hume have made natural theology
impossible.

So the Barthians, postmoderns, and liberals are all opposed
to natural theology. The great exceptions to these groups are
Roman Catholic theologians and the analytic philosophers

of religion. One of the undoubted strengths of the Roman Catholic tradition is its commitment to natural theology. They correctly perceive that there is much at stake. A God who does not make knowledge of God available to all God's creatures is not a loving or just God. If knowledge of God is confined exclusively to the Church, then given that the Church has only touched the lives of a small minority of humankind, the majority are deprived. Some form of natural theology is essential for the sake of theodicy.

So the great defenders of natural theology are the analytic philosophers of religion. Both here and in the United States, we have some very formidable philosophers defending the arguments in favour of the existence of God. One might expect this work to be received with some excitement by theologians. Instead, however, we find mutual bewilderment and incomprehension. The philosophers do not read the theologians. You will search in vain for a discussion of Jürgen Moltmann's account of God in the work of Richard Swinburne. Almost all of the philosophers confine their reading to the classical texts – Augustine, Anselm, Aquinas – and do not even mention contemporary writers, such as Pannenberg or Barth. And the theologians do not read the philosophers. The theologians get annoyed with the historical insensitivity and the often crude ways in which the Bible gets used. So in short the philosophers are fascinated by a narrow branch of natural theology, while the theologians totally ignore it.

There are several purposes of this book. First, I want to reinstate natural theology at the heart of all good theology. From St Paul in Romans 1, through to St Augustine and St Thomas, we find natural theology central. The Barthian and postmodern lack of interest in this way of thinking is a significant departure and, I would add, betrayal of the Christian tradition. Second, I want to encourage conversation between the analytical philosophers and the theologians. I have attempted to live in both of these worlds and value the achievements of both sides. This is a tricky position to be in: inevitably one will make mistakes in reporting the complexities of the internal debates within each discipline. This book

started out as the Boundy Lectures at the University of Exeter.
I then had a choice: either spend a further ten years in
intensive study to expand the book to six times its size or
offer the lectures to the academic community as a stimulating
(hopefully) and provocative (almost certainly) contribution
to the nature of God and our assumptions underpinning truth.
Although I am confident that each part of my argument can
be defended, I am conscious that I have not always done the
defending in sufficient depth or detail.

*The argument of the book attempts to demonstrate that 'critical
realism' depends on theism. It is developing and defending the
traditional argument, found in Augustine, from truth to God. The
initial chapters defend critical realism; the concluding chapters
illustrate that ultimately such a defence needs theism. In the end, I
believe that anybody who believes that it is possible to describe the
world in better or worse ways ought (logically) to believe in God.*
Many theists, let alone atheists, will find this shocking. This is
partly because we do not realize what being religious involves.
Both believers and non-believers have lost the all-embracing
nature of belief. Unlike Augustine and Nietzsche, they do
not understand just how radically different the world is if there
is no God.

The book has six chapters. In the first I outline a theological
description of what it means to be religious. It is an attempt
to locate the precise difficulty with Swinburne *et al.* If you
take certain paradigmatic theological expositors (say St Paul
and St Augustine) you find that their account of faith is
totally embracing; it is a total world perspective which explains
every facet of human life and existence. The problem with
Swinburne is that God looks like a tagged on extra. Atheists
and Christians can agree about much but not about this extra
'thing' called God. This is simply insufficient. As this sets the
scene for a book on natural theology, I attempt to show that
this 'all-embracing' nature of the religious world perspective
is not simply true of the Christian but of others in different
religious traditions.

In the second chapter, we start our exploration of the
nature of truth. Much of this chapter draws heavily on the
work of Alasdair MacIntyre. MacIntyre is one of the few

philosophers who is both trained in the analytic tradition and read widely by theologians. His historical sensitivity is finely honed and aware of the postmodern difficulties with a realist account of truth. In the third chapter, critical realism is defended. However, we leave that chapter with a major difficulty. Critical realism needs to assume the intelligibility of the world. How is this possible to justify? This becomes the task in the fourth chapter. It is here that the argument from truth to God is developed. Building on the work of Augustine and Anselm, I endorse a version of the cosmological argument as a justification of the intelligibility of the world.

In the fifth chapter, Friedrich Nietzsche is introduced as someone who would agree with the conclusion at the end of the fourth, but insists that we just 'cannot believe in God any-more'. He saw that once God goes, realism goes. We conclude that chapter aware of the choice: Nietzsche or Aquinas. In the last chapter I identify three implications of the argument, namely, the importance of natural theology, the inclusiveness of theism, and the centrality of process, rather than content, in Christian ethics.

Notes

1. James Barr, *Biblical Faith and Natural Theology* (Oxford: Clarendon Press, 1993), p. 1. This definition is wider, and there-fore more helpful, than the tendency of some philosophers of religion to confine natural theology to attempts to prove God's existence. However, as will become apparent in the book, I will be suggesting that natural theology should be seen as the 'explication of the theistic narrative'.
2. See, for example, George Newlands' excellent book, *Generosity and the Christian Future* (London: SPCK, 1997).
3. See Gareth Jones, *Critical Theology* (Cambridge: Polity Press, 1995), chapter 6.

CHAPTER 1

Being religious: what does this involve?

'A habit of basing convictions upon evidence, and of giving to them only that degree of certainty which the evidence warrants, would, if it became general, cure most of the ills from which the world is suffering.'[1] For Bertrand Russell, a little clear thinking would eliminate religion and, in so doing, eliminate much of the world's suffering. One senses in Russell total bewilderment at the whole phenomenon of religion. Beliefs such as life after death, explains Russell, simply do not make sense; there is no way people can survive the death of their brain. And a belief in a supreme being – a creator of the universe – simply lacks evidence. None of the traditional 'proofs' seem to justify belief, while the fact of evil provides a real reason for scepticism. So how does Russell explain the persistence of religion? He offers the following explanation:

> Religion is based, I think, primarily and mainly upon fear. It is partly the terror of the unknown, and partly . . . the wish to feel that you have a kind of elder brother who will stand by you in all your troubles and disputes. Fear is the basis of the whole thing – fear of the mysterious, fear of defeat, fear of death.[2]

Russell is a typical figure. He is typical of many in holding a view which betrays a lack of understanding of what being religious involves: for Russell, belief in God is a question of postulating a rather large object who started the universe. Such an object should be a matter of evidence; the arguments for and against this object should be capable of being weighed up and evaluated. We are being asked to speculate about

7

something that, even if it did exist, is probably unknowable. Humans should not expect to be able to resolve these large metaphysical questions. And agnosticism is confirmed by the fact that different religious traditions offer conflicting and contradictory accounts of this 'God'. Reason should incline us to agnosticism; it is the irrationality of faith that provokes belief.

Russell is right. Treat belief in God on the same level as belief in any other large mysterious object and belief becomes irrational. Consider the issue of the Loch Ness Monster: on the side of belief, there is a significant number of blurred pictures of a 'monster-type' creature; on the side of unbelief, there is the lack of decisive evidence, despite the use of sophisticated scientific equipment. Most reasonable people would agree that certainty would be inappropriate and that agnosticism is the position to take. Yet when it comes to God – a bigger and even more speculative object, such reasonableness disappears. On little or no evidence, believers claim complete certainty about their mutually incompatible gods.

One can respond to this problem illustrated by Russell in a variety of ways. The first accepts his understanding of religion but rejects his evaluation of the evidence. This is the position ably expressed by Richard Swinburne. I shall consider his position with care, but show that Swinburne, in the end, shares with Russell an irreligious view of religion. The second response to Russell makes much of the inappropriateness of his view of religion, but then suggests an alternative that most religious people do not recognize as a description of their faith. This response has been most ably explored by those influenced by Wittgenstein. I shall concentrate on the work of D. Z. Phillips. Against both of the responses of Swinburne and Phillips, I shall suggest an alternative that stresses the nature of religion as an all-embracing world-view (or – the term I prefer – world-perspective). On this view, religion is not a claim about an object in reality, but about the assumptions underlying our view of the nature of reality.

The task in this chapter is to formulate a religious view of religion – one that the great orthodox thinkers of most religious traditions would recognize. So the argument is in the end 'descriptive'. For it to succeed, I need to show that both Swinburne and Phillips are not capturing the heart of the 'religious experience' as felt by most religious believers. We start then with the first response.

Swinburne's response

The achievement of Richard Swinburne is considerable. For much of this century philosophy of religion concentrated on the odd nature of religious language, coupled with some discussion of the traditional proofs that Hume and Kant had demolished. Swinburne entirely rejected this position. His *The Coherence of Theism*, published in 1977, was a clarion call to philosophers to rediscover metaphysics.[3] His work coincided with the American Society of Christian Philosophers that shared the Swinburne agenda. Alvin Plantinga, Thomas Morris, Marilyn McCord Adams and Robert Merrihew Adams are all exceptionally rigorous philosophers who enjoy the business of traditional metaphysics. God was back as a genuine philosophical option.

Swinburne has written three books on this subject that set out his basic position. In *The Coherence of Theism* he delivers his account of religious language and defends the coherence of the idea of God. In *The Existence of God* he argues that there are good inductive arguments for the existence of his God. In *Faith and Reason* he argues that belief in the creed of Christianity, which he sees as having probability on its side, is sufficient for the practice of religion. I shall briefly outline the main contours of Swinburne's position.

On religious language, he follows the thirteenth-century philosopher and theologian John Duns Scotus.[4] Religious assertions take certain human concepts from mundane situations and stretch them out to apply to God. So the assertion 'God is love' takes the same basic human quality of 'concern for others' and stretches it out to apply to God. There is no need for St Thomas's tortured 'analogy' or Ian Ramsey's 'models and qualifiers'. God has certain qualities that are found amongst humans to a much greater degree. Just occasionally one finds oneself forced to the use of words in an analogical rather than direct way, but he stresses that this must be the last resort. Swinburne writes,

> [C]learly we ought to assume that theists are using words in their ordinary mundane senses . . . When the theist says that God is 'good', 'good' is, I suggest, being used in a perfectly ordinary sense. The only extraordinary thing being suggested is that it exists to a degree in which it does not exist in mundane objects. But when theists say that God is a 'person' who is 'necessarily' able to 'bring about' any state of affairs and 'knows' all things, I shall suggest that if what they say is to be coherent some of these words must be being used in somewhat analogical senses.[5]

Swinburne's intention is to stress the intelligibility of God-talk. Once we start creating unique rules for our language about God, which in principle humans are too finite to understand, then it becomes very difficult to distinguish gobbledygook from coherent talk; and religious talk becomes simply a creation of the imagination. And anyway, argues Swinburne, since it is possible to construct a metaphysic without too much analogy, then let us avoid needless complexity.

With this view of religious language, he then begins to formulate his definition of God. God is, explains Swinburne, 'like a person without a body (i.e. a spirit) who is eternal, free, able to do anything, knows everything, is perfectly good, is the proper object of human worship and obedience, the creator and sustainer of the universe'.[6] Swinburne clearly feels that he is defending the traditional picture of God. Certainly he wants to affirm all the traditional attributes, including God's omnipotence and omniscience. Although he modifies the traditional relation of God and time, he feels that this is a fairly minimalist adjustment for the sake of coherence.[7] However, I shall show that his 'personalist' view of God is a radical departure from the tradition; a departure that is fundamentally irreligious. But before so doing, let me continue my summary of Swinburne, by examining the evidence he adduces for the existence of his God.

Swinburne is selective in the arguments he is prepared to endorse. Among the traditional arguments, he dismisses the ontological argument completely, while only providing a very weak version of the cosmological argument. Instead he concentrates on the design argument and the argument from religious experience. On design, Swinburne is struck by the amazing consistency of the natural order: the fact that the laws of nature continue to operate from moment to moment. Clearly this fundamental consistency cannot be explained by science because science is only possible because natural laws are stable; therefore we need an alternative level of explanation. And this alternative explanation is a personal explanation.[8] On religious experience, Swinburne simply draws attention to the many millions of sane, well-balanced individuals who are totally convinced that they have experienced God. If these people were telling us of some everyday experience (such as seeing a mutual friend in the high street), we would be inclined to accept their report. They are not drunk; they do not take drugs; they are not given to spectacular story-telling; and they lack any motive to mislead. Yet when it comes to a metaphysical experience, we suddenly become so much more sceptical. This is unreasonable. We ought to concede that the widespread phenomenon of religious experience is good evidence for the reality of God.[9] In both cases – the arguments from design and religious experience – Swinburne wants us to accept them as good inductive arguments for the existence of God.

Swinburne has correctly identified certain factors that ought to be taken seriously by the sceptic. However, I want to suggest that these factors are a small part of the theistic world-perspective. God is not simply the best explanation, out of many possible explanations, for religious experience and natural order, but, as we shall see, a way of looking at the world that interprets everything differently. Swinburne's universe is the same as Russell; the only difference is that 'God exists'. God is an extra entity in the totality of things. To be fair to Swinburne, he does feel that this makes an enormous difference and, of course, God is the cause of everything that is. However, I want to suggest that the religious person wants to go further. Theism is not simply a claim about the existence of a 'God' but a world-view that leaves nothing untouched. In the end, Swinburne has failed to capture the all-embracing nature of the theistic claim.

To illustrate this, it is interesting to look at Swinburne's account of faith and reason. He begins by reminding us that the claim 'God exists' has the same character as any other scientific hypothesis. He draws an overt parallel with science and religion in the cause of criticism of Kant, who rejected theistic argument of this kind. He writes:

> The science of the last two centuries has told us of fields and forces and strange entities such as quarks and gluons underlying and causing observable phenomena. The grounds for believing the claims of science here are that science postulates entities in some respects simple, whose interactions lead us to expect the observable phenomena. Granted that the scientist has given good reason for believing in the existence of the entities which he postulates, there is no reason in principle to suppose that knowledge cannot advance so far as to explain the whole physical world, observable and unobservable, e.g. in terms of the action of a creator God.[10]

Once one arrives at such a concept of God, it generates a certain attitude to faith. Complete certainty is clearly inappropriate. For Swinburne, to believe that the proposition 'there is a God' is true means that one 'believes it more probable than any alternative'.[11] He then stresses that this uncertain faith ought to express itself in certain practices: he writes, 'The point of practicing religion is to secure one's own deepest well-being, or that of one's fellows, or that of God (in the respect that he is properly honoured and obeyed).'[12] Thus God is a scientific hypothesis that is probably true, which requires the observation of certain practices (for example, prayer and church attendance) and the cultivation of certain dispositions (for example, being more generous). Conversion, passion, conviction, and total love of God seem strangely inappropriate on Swinburne's account of faith. It is hardly the faith of Abraham, Isaac and Jacob. A scientific hypothesis requires a degree of detachment; as evolution explains the fossil record, so God explains the order of the universe; one should not become obsessed with evolution nor should one do so with God.

So the problem with Swinburne is not that he believes in an 'objective' God, but that this God 'object' is located as one object among many in the universe. Swinburne has treated God as a large, remarkable, strange, and very important object. This object is located at the edge of our experience. The disagreement with an atheist is simply a disagreement about the explanation for order in nature and religious experience. For the rest, one can agree with the sceptic about the nature of the world and the appropriate values one ought to accept; being religious simply involves an additional set of practices (i.e. practices of a religious kind) which are based upon the belief that a God is more probable than not, plus a certain strengthening of moral obligations.

The view of God as, in effect, a giant object is partly a result of his view of religious language. Swinburne's stress on intelligibility is entirely understandable and, in the light of much tortured modern theology, an appropriate corrective, but it ignores a fundamental feature of religious faith. This is the doctrine of creation, where the Creator is responsible for the creation. That must mean that God will be different from and other than the creation. Also it explains why Aquinas needs to find a middle way between intelligibility and mystery. For Aquinas, God-talk in relation to ordinary talk is not univocal (i.e. with words used with identical meanings in the two situations) nor is it equivocal (words used with completely unrelated meanings in the two situations) but analogical (words used with different yet related meanings in the two situations). So the idea that 'God is good' is linked with human goodness (in that, according to the analogy of attribution, it is sufficient to cause human goodness) yet simultaneously God's goodness is significantly different from human goodness. Aquinas requires that we should remove from our idea of God's goodness anything that implies imperfection or creaturely existence and think of God possessing these 'pure perfections' in a supereminent degree.[13] This is not needless complexity because it ensures that the otherness of God is protected. Aquinas's account of religious language clearly demonstrates that orthodox Christianity does not hold that God is a big person just above the clouds. The Creator, for Aquinas, enables all things to be, and exists in a way quite different from anything else that exists. Far from being simply an extension of ordinary usage, all human language about God will be an approximation, for the mystery of God will not permit complete human description.

When Paul Tillich suggested that religious language is symbolic, he was trying, in his own way, to protect both intelligibility and mystery. The same can be said for Ian Ramsey's idea of 'models' and 'qualifiers'. God is not to be viewed as a 'giant object': Ramsey writes, 'for the religious man "God" is a key word, an irreducible posit, an ultimate of explanation expressive of the kind of commitment he professes'.[14] In Swinburne's case, being religious involves a claim about a part of the universe; in Ramsey's case, being religious involves a claim about the entire universe. Ramsey is exactly right when he writes, 'So we see religious commitment as a total commitment to the whole universe . . .'[15]

Phillips' response

The subject of religious commitment leads us neatly into the second response to the Russell attack. For religious commitment has been a central theme in the work of D. Z. Phillips. A religious person's preoccupation with the reality of God is not a preoccupation with the origins of the universe. A religious person who dies for his or her faith is not dying for a religious hypothesis that on balance is more probable than not. Phillips writes, 'Strong belief is not tentative or hypothetical. Believers do not pray to a God who probably exists'.[16] He goes on to illustrate the point vividly with his alternative readings of Psalm 139. He writes:

> What would be a foundationalist reading of the psalm? 'Whither shall I go from thy Spirit? or whither shall I flee from thy presence? If I ascend up into heaven, it is highly probable that thou art there: if I make my bed in hell, behold it is highly probable that thou art there also?' The following

reading fares no better: 'If I ascend up into heaven, it is cumulatively apparent that thou are there; if I make my bed in hell, behold it is cumulatively apparent that thou art there also.' Surely, in the original the Psalmist testifies to the inescapable reality of God.[17]

Phillips makes much of the following apparently confused situation: religious people are totally certain and committed to the reality of God, yet any reasons given for faith are always less certain than their commitment would, on rational grounds, demand. If belief in God is treated in the Russell way – as a hypothesis about the start of the universe – then religious people are irrational, for rationally numerous difficulties and therefore doubts will always surround a highly speculative hypothesis such as this. Hence a religious person is not entitled to be completely certain.

Phillips relieves the confusion by drawing on the work of Ludwig Wittgenstein.[18] Wittgenstein argued that human discourse is a multi-faceted entity, and no single rationality can embrace its diversity. Instead of searching for one meta-rationality that provides rules of meaningfulness for all human discourse, one should concede that there are many different rationalities with different rules. He offers the analogy of language games. Consider soccer, cricket, patience, and chess: each game has a different set of rules. It would be absurd to ask a goalkeeper to checkmate the forward or to instruct a chess player to use the bishop to bowl an over. The mistake in both cases is that each game has its own set of rules and its own 'language'. You can only judge an activity within a game by the rules of that particular game. So by analogy, science and religion are separate language games. Within science one constructs an hypothesis and provides evidence for and against; in religion one does not do this. To ask the question: does God exist? within the rules of the scientific language game is as inappropriate as asking whether a knight is offside in chess.

Thus far this might all seem very reasonable. However, when Phillips comes to the implications of the language-game analogy, things become a little more complicated. To understand God-talk one needs to learn the language of religious

communities. According to Phillips, as one does this, one dis-
covers that religious people are not making straightforward
claims about reality; instead religious language is a way of
coping with the difficulties in life. So a prayer for a sick relative,
for example, is not supposed to bring healing to the patient.
If one does pray with that expectation, then one is guilty of
superstition, and this would not be authentic religion. It would
be a case of misapplying quasi-scientific procedures as if
religious dealings were comparable to asking the appropriate
human benefactor to intervene in one's situation of need. For
Phillips, when one understands the language of prayer from
within the language game of religion, then one sees that it is
really a way of coping with the contingencies of being human.

It is understandable why Phillips is so frequently described
as an 'anti-realist' in religion. Does God objectively exist?
Phillips' answer is exasperating; he seems to say 'yes' if you
are asking the question within the language game of religion,
and 'no' if you are asking it within the language game of
science. Yet life is not made up of these different unrelated
compartments. God's reality cannot be confined to a language
game. What started out as an exercise in understanding the
claims of religious people has ended up offering an account
that few religious persons would recognize.

Being religious: a proposal

Being religious is not simply a claim about part of the world
nor is it a matter of living within a language game of its own.
Instead I shall show that, if you take the account of faith found
in the great theologians, the most important feature of a
religious world-view is its all-embracing character. I shall argue
that 'being religious' involves three key features: these are
(1) a claim about the nature of all reality, (2) an all-embracing
world-view that contrasts markedly with the secular humanist
one, and (3) a certain set of assumptions that touch everything. I shall develop these three features.

One tempting way to resolve problems within theism is to
insist that 'believing in God' is not a claim about reality, but

simply a way of looking at the world, as Phillips appears to be holding. Don Cupitt, for example, defines God as: 'the sum of our values, representing to us their ideal unity, their claims upon us and their creative power'.[19] The Church, on this account, becomes a setting in which we can think-through our values. God is simply the claim that certain moral values ought to be making of us.

We need not be detained further by the details of Cupitt's proposals,[20] and I shall take issue with his anti-realism in chapter two. Suffice it to say that the main difficulty with his proposal is his sanguine acceptance of the naturalist world-view. In removing God from reality, he leaves reality as cold, impersonal, and ultimately reducible to bundles of atoms. Metaphysics is still there in Cupitt; it is now the metaphysics of naturalism. But a religious world-view is one that makes a claim about reality. This claim about reality is best put negatively: religious people want to insist that one cannot make sense of the complexity of reality simply in terms of impersonal atoms. The vast majority of cultures (both historically and today) share a view that runs counter to the modern scientific, secular, and humanist world-view. Love, morality, art, music, beauty, and our religious intuitions are taken to point to the personal nature of reality.

The comparison between the all-embracing religious world-view and a secular humanist world-view forms the basis of my second factor.[21] However, I think that it is preferable to talk of 'world-perspective' rather than 'world-view'.[22] Both terms capture the essential point that we come to the world and understand it through a certain framework. But the term 'world-view' may sound as if it were a matter of certain propositions, and discovering one's world-view no more than a rational, empiricist exercise. This ignores the fact that all of us have a world-perspective; one that we start to discover from the moment of birth: it includes economic power, race, gender, language, values, and sexuality. I speak as a middle-class, white, Western Christian working in a British University and, of course, I look at the world differently from a poor Asian Hindu woman trying to survive in the slums of Calcutta. Yet although there are numerous differences between us,

there are certain things we share. First, we both have a perspective on a 'world', that is, horizons stretching out beyond
ourselves; and second, we both share a religious world-
perspective that is opposed to the secular humanist one. In
other words, while the Asian Hindu woman might find me
odd, she would find Bertrand Russell even odder.

The odd thing about Russell is his total, complacent acceptance of the reductionist scientific world-perspective. He sets
out his assumptions, when he writes:

> That Man is the product of causes which had no prevision of the
> end they were achieving; that his origin, his growth, his hopes
> and fears, his loves and his beliefs, are but the outcome of
> accidental collocations of atoms; that no fire, no heroism, no
> intensity of thought and feeling, can preserve an individual life
> beyond the grave; that all the labours of the ages, all the devotion,
> all the inspiration, all the noonday brightness of human genius,
> are destined to extinction in the vast death of the solar system,
> and that the whole temple of Man's achievement must inevitably
> be buried beneath the debris of a universe in ruins – all these
> things, if not quite beyond dispute, are yet so nearly certain,
> that no philosophy which rejects them can hope to stand. Only
> within the scaffolding of these truths, only on the firm foundation
> of unyielding despair, can the soul's habitation henceforth be
> safely built.[23]

For Russell, the whole emergence of life is blind chance. When
Russell looks at the world, he sees the chance phenomenon
of an expanding universe that had within it the factors to
generate life. After a long struggle, certain life forms developed consciousness. And as death comes to all creatures
so comes extinction. And, finally, the entire edifice of life will
probably disappear in the death of the entire solar system.
Such is the naturalist world-perspective, which itself may carry
certain implications for behaviour. Questions such as 'why
not pursue self-interest in every situation?' have a certain force,
which can only be answered by the personal decision to opt
for altruism.

Those of us with a religious world-perspective find Russell
rather strange. We have a different framework within which
to view life. I shall, now, briefly sketch this alternative frame-

work. We share the insights offered by scientists on the mechanics of the story, but see these mechanics as a part of a greater whole. The cause, the heart, and the hope of the universe are goodness and love. This is what a theist means by God. God is a being that causes all things to be, who has the characteristics of personhood in that s/he can decide, feel, act, and is good. It is an optimistic view of the universe. The universe on this account is not ultimately inanimate, but personal.[24] It is in the nature of love that it needs to create more possibilities for personal relations whereby love can find expression and fruition. Thus it is in the nature of love to create. As the universe expanded, the drive was always towards the emergence of life. All life is significant (plants as well as animals), but humans are distinctive because their self-consciousness, intelligence and language mean that they have been given the capacity to give and receive love. As we discover and create loving relationships, we discover that which really matters; we discover that which will survive for eternity. For love cannot be defeated by death. The basic religious impulse of worship will appear puzzling if one sees God as a super-person operating to create and uphold the universe. To worship this big person would be idolatry. The Hebrew Bible insists on the otherness of God from the creation because God is not in mere conformity with the creation. Worship is not pandering to a giant ego and telling 'him' how wonderful he is. Instead it is the recognition that God is the source of everything we value. In placing ultimate value on God as the source of all that is love and good, so we place appropriate value on everything else.

Worship forces one to monotheism. This is no doubt partly due to the fact that given the choice of the 'One' or the 'Many', then the One is a simpler explanation. But it is also due to the discernment of an ultimate unity made possible through worship. There cannot be a plurality of ultimate beings; a being cannot be ultimate if it is one of many. It is no co-incidence that all the major world religions have a strong tendency towards monotheism. Furthermore, worship for the theist should have ethical implications. This is the reason why the prophet Amos insisted that authentic worship must be reflected in appropriate political values. We cannot worship God (i.e. affirm that which is good) while oppressing our neighbour (i.e. act in ways that are wicked). It is a contradiction.[25]

It might seem that this account of the 'religious' world-perspective is not 'religious' in a general way at all, instead it is 'Christian'. It is certainly true that I am a Christian. And I could develop the account offered above in certain ways and make it distinctively Christian. So the significance of God as 'love at the heart of all that is' means that God also must be in relation, for you cannot have solitary love. This is one of the main reasons why Christians talk of God as a Trinity. And the impossibility of love being defeated by death is the major theological significance of the resurrection of Jesus. Yet these themes (using different language, stories, and events) can also be found in the other major world faiths. It is not to say that all religions are the same. Such a claim is as false as saying 'Christianity has absolutely nothing in common with other religions'. Instead the truth is that all religious traditions do share an antagonism to secular humanism (hence the initial stress on the negative objective claim made by the religious world-perspective) and certain strands of each tradition do share an emphasis on the centrality of love.

Keith Ward has shown that accounts of religion offered by the 'orthodox' proponents of Christianity, Islam, Judaism, Hinduism, and Buddhism have much in common. The basic structure of faith, as conceived by the leading writers within each tradition, has a basic similarity. At the heart of each tradition is the iconic vision: it is a way of looking at the world that discerns the infinite through the finite. The iconic vision, Ward writes, is 'a vision of the temporal in the light of eternity'.[26] This vision is not a theoretical reflection on the world but requires a decision in terms of life-style and behaviour. The life-style decision Ward calls 'the self-transcending response'. He illustrates the different exemplary roles and models that are found in each tradition, all requiring this response, when he writes:

It is my self which must become an icon of the self-manifesting God. I can indeed see him as the glorified Lord whom I can revere as over against me. I can see him as the one who is hidden in all finite things, and thus see Christ in every other person, as an object of reverence and care. But I must also, and first of all, allow Christ to live in me, transforming my mind into the likeness of him until I can say, with Paul, 'Not I live, but Christ lives in me' (Gal. 2:20). Or, in other traditions, I must allow the Buddha-nature to grow in me; I must let the true Self come to realization in me; I must let the Torah grow in my heart and soul, until I am filled with the spirit of God; or I must submit my life wholly to Allah, until 'all perishes save his countenance', and his will is perfectly worked out through my obedience.[27]

Each tradition is requiring the transcendent to transform us. Each tradition is making certain life-style demands.

The heart of religion, then, is an iconic vision that requires a 'self-transcending response'. The doctrine of God arises when one tries to make sense of a religious view of reality. It is because the iconic vision involves the eternal and unknown becoming temporal and manifest in some way that one finds 'a dual aspect doctrine of God'.[28] Ward explains the concept as follows:

> Philosophical fashions come and go; but the classical concept of God has an enduring validity. It presents the idea of God as infinite being, knowledge and bliss . . . It is self-existent and simple, not containing internal complexities, and thus utterly distinct from the complex world of name and form. Yet it is an essential part of the classical concept that God both causes and enters into finitude and an endless creative temporality, ever realizing new values in time . . . Dual-aspect theism is the classical view; it is present in every major religious tradition.[29]

This is a striking claim. At the heart of the major world faiths is the same basic structure. It does not mean that there is nothing distinctive in the different world religions, nor does it imply that there are no significant disagreements. But it does mean that the major world faiths are agreed not only in certain structural characteristics but also, fundamentally, in their witness to the error of secular humanism. So the fundamental decision is whether one is religious or not: whether one opts for a naturalist or secular humanist world-perspective or a religious one.

So to start summing up: Russell and Swinburne are both a long way from the 'orthodox' traditional understanding of God, though appearing at first sight to be radically opposed with regard to religious claims; they share a picture of religion woefully inadequate to the heart of religion. Yet this picture of religion is dominating popular Western culture. The question of God's existence is treated on the same level as questions about other mysterious entities: there might be a Loch Ness Monster; creatures might live in outer space; and there might be an alarmingly powerful entity called God who started the entire universe and may be our big brother, supervisor or judge.

Religious commitment is totally demanding because the religious world-perspective is all-embracing. God is not an appendage belief topping up or crowning all our other beliefs about reality: it is that in the absence (or presence) of which all beliefs are changed. It is a way of looking at the world that has profound implications for behaviour and attitudes of every kind, even to the most prosaic and everyday aspects of the world we encounter.

The religious perspective stresses the way in which everything is touched. The religious world-perspective is all pervasive. It not only tells a story about our past, present, and future; it not only provides a perspective into which everything fits; but it makes certain demands upon our behaviour.

Being religious and natural theology

In the next three chapters I propose to develop a version of natural theology: that is, attempts to establish the reality of God through reason, unaided by revelation. My aim has been to establish an appropriate understanding of the character of religion, such an understanding being essential to my subsequent task. Phillips complains that natural theology assumes God is an object, and points to Swinburne to prove his point. Although Phillips is correct to complain about Swinburne, it will be my contention that both have misunderstood the nature of natural theology.

'Being religious' involves holding a life-transforming, all-embracing world-perspective. Natural theology attempts to explicate and clarify the religious world-perspective. It is in the first instance a description, not a justification. For if natural theology were a justification, then it would have to share the same assumptions as the atheist. But the two world-perspectives of religion and secular humanism are so contrasting, that this essential common ground is not available. Yet as natural theology describes the religious world-perspective, it identifies precisely what is at stake.[30]

In the next two chapters I shall show that the secularist and the theist disagree about the possibility of truth. It is my purpose to show that truth is only defensible if one believes in God. Take away God and there is no adequate safeguard against nihilism and scepticism. We have, in short, a straight choice: Nietzsche or Aquinas – to take my preferred defender of theism. Belief in God is so fundamental that it affects absolutely everything. We cannot even be sure that true statements are possible once God goes.

Notes

1. B. Russell, *Why I am not a Christian* (London: Unwin, 1967), p. 10.
2. Ibid., p. 25.
3. Richard Swinburne, *The Coherence of Theism* (Oxford: Clarendon Press, 1977). See his introduction.
4. Ibid., pp. 72f.
5. Ibid., p. 71.
6. Ibid., p. 1.
7. For Swinburne time is a part of God: so there is succession and duration within the Almighty.
8. See Richard Swinburne, *The Existence of God* (Oxford: Clarendon Press, 1979), chapter 8.
9. See ibid., chapter 13.

10. Richard Swinburne, *Faith and Reason* (Oxford: Clarendon Press, 1981), p. 83. This is a summary of conclusions he formulates at greater length in *The Existence of God*, chapter 3.
11. Richard Swinburne, *Faith and Reason*, p. 119.
12. Ibid., p. 138.
13. See Eric Mascall's excellent discussion of Aquinas's view of religious language in *Existence and Analogy* (London: Darton, Longman & Todd, 1949).
14. Ian T. Ramsey, *Religious Language* (London: SCM Press, 1957), p. 47.
15. Ibid., p. 37.
16. D. Z. Phillips, *Faith After Foundationalism* (London and New York: Routledge, 1988), p. xiii.
17. Ibid., pp. 9f. Phillips is thinking of Richard Swinburne for the first reading and Basil Mitchell for the second.
18. There is considerable disagreement about Wittgenstein's views on religion. However, for an excellent report on 'language games', I have found Kenny's discussion very helpful. See A. Kenny, *Wittgenstein* (London: Penguin, 1973), chapter 10.
19. Don Cupitt, *The Sea of Faith* (London: BBC, 1984), p. 269.
20. The difficulties with the Cupitt project have been ably explored by Keith Ward, *Holding Fast To God* (London: SPCK, 1982) and Brian Hebblethwaite, *The Ocean of Truth* (Cambridge: Cambridge University Press, 1988).
21. John Hick makes much of the idea that faith is an interpretative process that sees theism as the best explanation for all human life. The account that follows shares Hick's approach to a degree, the difference is that I do not think this excludes natural theology. For John Hick, see *Faith and Knowledge* (London: Fount, 1957).
22. See my 'World Perspectives and Arguments: Disagreements about Disagreements', *Heythrop Journal*, 30 (1) 1989: 1–12.
23. Bertrand Russell, *Mysticism and Logic* (London: Longmans, 1919).
24. This account of God is heavily influenced by process theology. Although the doctrine of creation involves a God apart from the creation, it is important to stress the links between God and the world.
25. This account of worship is an attempt to summarize the picture provided in the orthodox and most developed strands of the theistic traditions. Naturally, in among the almost infinite variety

of traditions, there will be those who would endorse the superstitious or non-ethical accounts of worship.

26. Keith Ward, *Images of Eternity* (Oxford: Oneworld, 1987), p. 165.
27. Ibid., pp. 153–4.
28. Ward uses the term 'God' with apologies to Buddhism. Although he finds the same structure in Buddhism, he recognizes that it would not use the terminology of theism. For Ward's apology see ibid., p. viii, and for Ward's discussion of Buddhism see chapter 3.
29. Ibid., pp. 155–6.
30. Basil Mitchell in his book, *The Justification of Religious Belief* (London: Macmillan Press, 1973) distinguishes between strict proof (presumably deductive arguments), arguments from probability and his own 'cumulative' arguments. He suggests in the same way that one might argue for an interpretation of a text or a historical event, so one can construct in a similar way an argument for a theistic interpretation of the world. He correctly sees that one is not arguing from a part of the world to another object within the world, but to a total world-view. So he writes, '[T]raditional Christian theism may be regarded as a world-view or metaphysical system which is in competition with other such systems and must be judged by its capacity to make sense of all the available evidence' (p. 99). Mitchell believes that this description of theism makes 'more sense' than all alternatives. Although I would not go that far, I am suggesting that we need to see natural theology as a description of our world-perspective, which might persuade because of its comprehensive nature, rather than a justification from shared assumptions to belief in God.

CHAPTER 2

Truth and MacIntyre

In the first chapter I argued that 'being religious' involves a total commitment to a theistic world perspective. Instead of a universe emerging by chance within which everything faces ultimate oblivion, theists believe that the universe is a result of purpose and love, and intended for the realization and creation of further loving possibilities. Put like this, it sounds as if the difference between the naturalist and theist is not that great. The naturalist tends towards pessimism, while the theist is more optimistic; the naturalist thinks it is just being realistic, while the theist is more hopeful.

I shall now show that the difference is much more significant. It extends to the possibility of truth. Over the next four chapters I shall show that the assumptions underpinning a critical-realist account of truth need to be grounded in theism. Once God goes, the possibility of truth is undermined. But first we need to clarify precisely what we mean by truth. Over the next two chapters I shall develop an account of truth that takes seriously the problems many philosophers have with critical realism. In my judgement the philosopher who has done most to confront the whole range of historicist problems is Alasdair MacIntyre. He will figure prominently in the next three chapters. For in broad outline, MacIntyre provides the framework for the account of truth that I shall defend. To understand the achievement of MacIntyre, it is necessary to examine the traditional philosophical debate on truth and briefly identify the main difficulties.

Truth

What do we mean by 'truth'? Inevitably this question has attracted considerable discussion by philosophers: so the purpose of this discussion is confined to illustrating the distinctive approach of MacIntyre compared to those in mainstream philosophy.[1] Discussion of contemporary philosophy will inevitably be selective.

Most introductions to philosophy offer four main options.[2] The first is the correspondence theory of truth. This is probably closest to what most people mean by truth in ordinary speech. Truth is the property of corresponding to reality. So 'it is raining' is true, if, when looking out of the window, I see rain falling. In this case a belief (which can take the form of a statement, sentence, proposition) is true when there exists a fact corresponding with it. However, the theory needs to be supplemented with a clear account of what facts are and what exactly it means to correspond. And this is the point at which it runs into problems. So what is the precise relation between the claim that 'it is raining' to the reality of rain? How do we bridge the gap between my belief that it is raining and the fact in reality that it is raining? Several standard arguments for scepticism can be introduced at this point: at the most extreme, it is possible we might be dreaming. More interestingly, we all know that a stick placed in water appears bent, so we know that our senses can be misled. This gap between reality and the mental interpretations of reality is, for many philosophers, too difficult for the correspondence theory to bridge.[3]

The second and third options both eliminate the need for a correspondence with reality. Thus, the second theory stresses instead the importance of coherence. Truth is linked to statements. Statements are part of a system. The statements within the system must cohere with each other. The language of untruth is used when one offers a statement that does not fit in with others within the system. Internal consistency within a system is the only possible requirement for truth that one can set. This means that a tribal culture which explains illness in terms of spirits, and a scientific culture which offers

molecular explanations are both coherent options and therefore both true.[4]

The third theory seeks to supplement coherence with
'utility'.[5] What is required is not only an internally consistent
world-view, but one that 'works' in a pragmatic sense.[6]

The fourth view has a variety of names – the disquotational
notion, the redundancy view, or (the one preferred by the
most capable recent defender, Paul Horwich) the minimalist
theory. This account simplifies matters considerably: truth is
a synonym for that which is true. It is a way of saying: consider
x, x is true means x.[7]

It is odd how these options are still set out without any
historical setting. All too frequently the philosopher's preoccupation with ideas disregards the historical context. It is
in this sense that MacIntyre's contribution to philosophy is
enormously significant. The achievement of his *A Short History
of Ethics*[8] was that he located and attempted to explicate why
some of the apparently 'timeless' theories he was describing
emerged at certain points in history. So the emotivist theories
of ethics advocated by the logical positivists reflected a certain
historical and cultural shift – namely, the modern turn to the
subject and the inability to understand how to defend the
objectivity of moral assertions. Since *A Short History of Ethics*,
MacIntyre has developed further narratives to explain chang-
ing attitudes to both ethics and rationality.

We shall examine the ways in which MacIntyre illustrates
the 'tradition-constituted' nature of rationality later in this
chapter. Here I shall attempt a brief narrative that explains
the debate surrounding truth. In the Western tradition, it
was Aristotle, perhaps developing Plato's reflections in the
Sophist, who offered the basic form of the correspondence
theory of truth.[9] With significant variations, the basic insight
was affirmed throughout the medieval period. Both Augustine
and Aquinas formulate fairly sophisticated versions of the
theory.

It was the Enlightenment that created the problems. Kant,
building on Hume and Descartes, is responsible for the
perceived difficulties with correspondence. Where Augustine
had felt that the problems of perception do not undermine

the possibility of correspondence with reality, Kant saw the unbridgeable gap.[10] Kant is best understood in the light of Descartes and Hume. Descartes had created the impossible standard, that knowledge requires complete certainty.[11] Hume had shown that any attempt to meet that condition is doomed to failure.[12] Kant's solution is to distinguish between the noumenal and the phenomenal. The noumenal is the way things are in themselves; the phenomenal is the way things appear to mind. Despite the fact that much of Kant reads as if he is suggesting two separate worlds, most contemporary Kantian scholars believe that in fact he sees the noumenal and the phenomenal as part of the same world.[13] Kant is, to use Devitt's terminology, holding a minimal doctrine of 'weak, or Fig-Leaf, Realism'.[14] So it is not that the noumenal causes the phenomenal (two worlds), but that the phenomenal is the only way we can know the noumenal (one world). For Kant, the act of knowing involves both the actual object and the mental imposition of *a priori* categories along with the spatio-temporal setting. The problem when it comes to truth is that the mental in a very significant way is actually creating the world in which we live. Once this was seen, then consistency with the rational interpretative scheme became much more important. And if consistency matters, then coherence becomes central.

The pragmatist adjustment reflects a concern to explain change. Why adjust from one coherent scheme into another? The pragmatism of William James stresses the expedience of truth.[15] On this view science and, for James, religion are true because they work. They reap benefits in terms of quality of life.

This historical sensitivity creates the awareness that philosophical decisions about truth are not simply judgements about the plausibility of each account (in itself a very difficult exercise), but raises the question whether the cultural presuppositions of each account are justified. So the attractiveness of a coherence or pragmatist account of truth depends on the legitimacy of Kant, which in turn depends on the standard set by Descartes. This was MacIntyre's discovery in *Whose Justice? Which Rationality?*, where he shows brilliantly that the modern tendency towards relativism is a result of un-reasonable requirements for knowledge.

At this point MacIntyre needs expounding at some length. In this discussion, I shall locate MacIntyre in his own writing context, first by looking at the exchange between him and Winch earlier in his career, and then by examining his ideas in the light of Milbank's highly illuminating account in *Theology and Social Theory*.

MacIntyre and Winch

The exchange between Peter Winch and Alasdair MacIntyre arose in the context of anthropology. In 1958 Peter Winch had published a study called *The Idea of a Social Science*,[16] which MacIntyre rebutted in 1964. In 1970 Bryan Wilson published the articles involved in this disagreement, as a section in *Rationality*.[17]

Winch's starting point is the simple and obvious problem that there is no such thing as uninterpreted data. We cannot stand outside our particular cultural outlook and decide what the world is really like. We are all born into families, and families are parts of communities and cultures. The way we look at the world is partly determined by the cultural in-fluences that determine the interpretation of that world.

Ludwig Wittgenstein was, in his later work, extremely sensi-tive to the different cultures and 'language games' in the world. In the same way that each game has a different set of rules so has each culture. One cannot be checkmate in a game of basketball for that is to confuse the rules of two different games. So, argued Wittgenstein, it is equally inappropriate to use scientific language in a religious context or for that matter to judge a non-scientific culture by a scientific Western rationality.[18]

This argument is developed by Wittgenstein's disciple Peter Winch in such a way to show that comparison between cultures is impossible. If we attempt to compare two different cultures, we will either try to find an objective, external vantage point from which we can decide between the two cultures, or we will end up imposing the standards of our own culture. The attempt to stand outside our own culture is doomed to failure. We are who we are. We were born into a particular family and community, and have lived in a certain way. The quest for objectivity is illusory and fruitless. Yet the other option is clearly illegitimate also. To impose the standards of one's own culture is a form of imperialism. How do we know that our standards are the right ones? We do not, because we cannot transcend our situation to find out what the world is *really* like or not like.

The implications of this argument are extensive. Consider the following example that is discussed by both MacIntyre and Winch. 'According to Spencer and Gillen some aborigines carry about a stick or a stone which is treated as if it is or embodies the soul of the individual who carries it. If the stick or stone is lost, the individual anoints himself as the dead are anointed.'[19]

Now MacIntyre argues that such a practice is incoherent. One's identity is not linked to a stone, and it makes no sense to anoint oneself as dead unless one is dead. For Winch this is completely illegitimate:

> MacIntyre does not say why he regards the concept of carrying one's soul about with one in a stick as 'thoroughly incoherent'. He is presumably influenced by the fact that it would be hard to make sense of an action like this if performed by a twentieth-century Englishman or American; and by the fact that the soul is not a material object like a piece of paper and cannot, therefore, be carried about in a stick as a piece of paper might be.[20]

Winch goes on to suggest that the aboriginal practice is not even that strange from the Western perspective.

> Consider that a lover in our society may carry about a picture or lock of hair of the beloved . . . Suppose that when the lover loses the locket he feels guilty and asks his beloved for her forgiveness: there might be a parallel here to the aboriginal's practice of anointing himself when he 'loses his soul'. And is there necessarily anything irrational in these practices?[21]

To Winch, MacIntyre is importing his own cultural standards and imposing a crude scientific rationalism on a different cultural practice. Winch believes that this is totally improper. Why should a different culture be judged by our cultural standards? MacIntyre uses the laws of logic as if the whole world knows that they are valid. Winch explains:

> [C]riteria of logic are not a direct gift of God, but arise out of, and are only intelligible in the context of, ways of living or modes of social life as such. For instance, science is one such mode and religion is another; and each has criteria of intelligibility peculiar to itself. So within science or religion actions can be logical or illogical: in science, for example, it would be illogical to refuse to be bound by the results of a properly carried out experiment; in religion it would be illogical to suppose that one could pit one's strength against God's; and so on. But we cannot sensibly say that either the practice of science itself or that of religion is either illogical or logical; both are non-logical.[22]

Winch simply applies what he says of science and religion to the imposition of our own science-influenced cultural values on the aboriginals.

Winch has used a Wittgensteinian analysis to arrive at an anti-realist conclusion, that is, that the human mind cannot transcend its particular frame of reference and know which assertions correspond to reality. Others have arrived at the same conclusion through historicism – a sensitivity to the historical setting of all ideas, so that talk of the absolute truth is seen as impossible to justify.[23] Richard Rorty suggests that to judge another culture or to judge certain strands of one's own culture from the vantage point of a different tradition is the mistake of Philosophy (with a capital P).[24] It is the philosophy of the metaphysics that Hume and Kant long ago destroyed.

MacIntyre, responding to Winch, emphasizes the areas where he agrees with him. Each person is indeed born into a 'rule-governed' setting and, to begin with, activities need to be understood from within that setting. However, he rejects the Winch dichotomy. MacIntyre writes, 'For there are not two alternatives: either embracing the metaphysical fiction of one over-all "norm for intelligibility in general" or flying to total relativism.'[25] MacIntyre wants to take seriously the fact of our historical-cultural setting, but not to surrender the principles of rationality. This quest for a way through the middle between the Winch alternatives has become the dominant theme of MacIntyre's work. He takes up Winch's claims that cultural relativity makes it impossible to ask truth questions, for example, whether the Zande beliefs about witches are true?[26] MacIntyre develops Winch thus:

> We can ask from within the Zande system of beliefs if there are witches and will receive the answer 'Yes'. We can ask from within the system of beliefs of modern science if there are witches and will receive the answer 'No'. But we cannot ask which system of beliefs is the superior in respect of rationality and truth; for this would be to invoke criteria which can be understood independently of any particular way of life, and on Winch's view there are no criteria.[27]

Now, MacIntyre goes on, this creates two major problems. First, Winch has made it impossible to explain historical transitions. For example, in seventeenth-century Scotland there was a transition from a culture that believed in witches to one that did not. The determining question was one which Winch thinks impossible, namely, 'Are there really witches?' Those living at the time believed that they were moving to a world-view that was more accurate than the previous world-view. Winch makes this impossible, thereby making any historical narrative in these terms unintelligible.

The second problem is that translation becomes impossible. MacIntyre writes:

> Consider the statement made by some Zande theorist or by King James VI and I, 'There are witches', and the statement made by some modern sceptic, 'There are no witches'. Unless one of these statements denies what the other asserts, the negation of the sentence expressing the former could not be a translation of the sentence expressing the latter. Thus if we could not deny from our own standpoint and in our own language what the Azande or King James assert in theirs, we should be unable to translate their expression into our language. Cultural idiosyncrasy would have entailed linguistic idiosyncrasy and cross-cultural comparison would have been rendered logically impossible. But of course translation is not impossible.[28]

Translation is extremely important in the debate concerning relativism and truth. This passage from MacIntyre is particularly interesting as he develops the position in a much more ambiguous way in *Whose Justice? Which Rationality?* The argument from translation is, in my judgement, important for the position I shall defend towards the end of this chapter, and I save the extended discussion of this point for that section. Suffice it to say, I think the early MacIntyre is correct, and insofar as modification is needed then it is only slight.

However, at this stage in MacIntyre's career, the argument against Winch has consisted of an appeal to unacceptable consequences of the relativist's position. We had to wait until MacIntyre's *Whose Justice? Which Rationality?* for a suggested procedure for deciding between traditions. Here he distinguishes two different but related objections: the relativist challenge and the perspectivist challenge. MacIntyre explains:

> The relativist challenge rests upon a denial that rational debate between and rational choice among rival traditions is possible; the perspectivist challenge puts in question the possibility of making truth-claims from within any one tradition. For if there is a multiplicity of rival traditions, each with its own characteristic modes of rational justification internal to it, then that very fact entails that no one tradition can offer those outside it good reasons for excluding the theses of its rival. Yet if this is so, no one tradition is entitled to arrogate to itself an exclusive title; no one tradition can deny legitimacy to its rivals.[29]

Relativism, argues MacIntyre, arises when people try to insist that rational evaluation of conflicting traditions is only possible when standing outside these traditions; then, since this is impossible, relativism appears as the only option. MacIntyre commends a different approach. He calls it 'tradition-constituted and tradition-constitutive enquiry'.[30] This approach rejects the expectations of the relativist. It does this in two very important ways: (1) by not expecting to find a neutral standard; and (2) by not expecting to arrive at an all-embracing truth which would be an absolute truth. Underpinning the objections of the relativist is the problem of false expectations. These false expectations have arisen because of the Enlightenment. The Enlightenment project was an unattainable quest for absolute certainty. It is a modern post-Enlightenment problem.

Our current crisis is compared by MacIntyre with the development of certain pre-Enlightenment traditions. Within the histories of these traditions, MacIntyre believes the principles of tradition-constituted enquiry are expressed. For example, Aquinas did not have a belief in neutral vantage points transcending the various conflicting traditions surrounding us, but he still managed to make certain 'rational' judgements. In Aquinas there are two conflicting traditions that are engaged in debate and ultimately synthesized. He harmonizes an Aristotelian structure with an Augustinian psychology. Using this as one example, MacIntyre's entire book is a study of the principles of engagement between traditions within a historical and cultural framework. How is this possible?

Initially, traditions are founded within a community. A tradition can be said to begin when particular beliefs, institutions, and practices are articulated by certain people and/or in certain texts. In such a community authority will be conferred on these texts and voices. In discussing these texts, procedures for inquiry will be established. A rationality will develop. Problems for the community arise for any of the following reasons: one, when there are different and incompatible interpretations; two, when incoherences and inadequacies are identified; and three, when there is a confrontation with different systems.[31] When these problems arise, the community faces 'an epistemological crisis'.[32] The term 'epistemological crisis' describes a state where the traditional modes of inquiry are generating problems which the tradition lacks the resources to solve. Such a crisis itself generates the need for an imaginative conceptual innovation,[33] which gives rise to new beliefs that can be compared and contrasted with the older and less adequate beliefs. Such a comparison obviously requires a standard. Here MacIntyre outlines a variation on the correspondence theory of truth.[34] Ultimately, such traditions are trying to explain reality in as comprehensive a way as possible. Truth is ultimately achieved when the beliefs correspond with reality.

A tradition is successfully maintained if it can be shown that any proposed modification in belief and outlook can be demonstrated to stand in continuity with the rest of the tradition. It is possible that during an epistemological crisis, arising as a result of a conflict with another tradition, the adherents may decide that the new tradition is more appropriate than the earlier one. This is crucial. *MacIntyre believes that it is possible for one tradition when engaging another, to find that the other has better conceptual tools to understand human life and activity. A tradition can founder.* Although there is no neutral rationality to appeal to, the adherents of an existing tradition can come to find a different tradition's rationality more plausible. A judgement has been made between the two traditions. MacIntyre suggests that the developments leading to the science of Newton and Galileo might be of this type.[35]

Naturally, this engagement between traditions is not easy. Communication requires a common language, and language presupposes a rationality. MacIntyre believes that the only way for two traditions, with two different languages, to have dialogue, is for the participants to learn a second first-language. This term captures the necessity of learning the language as we did our first language when children. It is not simply a matter of matching sentences from our first language with our second, but of living and thinking with the concepts within the second language. This MacIntyre argues is both possible and necessary. And it enables movement within traditions and from (what comes to seem) one tradition to another to take place.

MacIntyre and Milbank

MacIntyre's project in *Whose Justice? Which Rationality?* is to find a way to stand within a tradition and yet make judgements between traditions. His position offers an attractive synthesis of historicism and the correspondence theory of truth.[36] John Milbank, in his *Theology and Social Theory*, argues that MacIntyre's position is ultimately untenable.[37] Milbank shares

MacIntyre's rejection of an overarching liberal, secular, rationality. However, Milbank goes on,

> MacIntyre, of course, wants to argue against this stoic-liberal-nihilist tendency, which is 'secular reason'. But my case is rather that it is only a mythos, and therefore cannot be refuted, but only out-narrated, if we persuade people – for reasons of 'literary taste' – that Christianity offers a much better story.[38]

Milbank argues that the problem with MacIntyre is that he is insufficiently historicist. The possibility of living in two traditions does not provide the means of deciding between the traditions, rather both traditions become a part of the person and will coexist in awkward tension.[39] Further, Milbank finds implausible the idea of a switch in traditions being legitimated according to the criteria of the older tradition, as MacIntyre's proposal indicated. It makes no sense to imagine a switch in 'rationalities' being determined by the rationality which is becoming obsolete. And finally, Milbank writes, 'It is similarly impossible to adjudicate the claim to "explain more"'. Movements in traditions, say from the Aristotelian to the Newtonian, 'have to be interpreted as essentially "rhetorical victories"'.[40]

Milbank, however, is not a straightforward anti-realist. He uses historicism to show that secular liberal rationality is one of several possible narratives, all of which rest on 'theological assumptions'. In a superb discussion of Nietzsche, he shows that the implications of this rationality are highly unsatisfactory and within it what actually occurs is the victory of the most powerful. Instead, Milbank suggests the following alternative: it is true that all we have is a range of different traditions, and decisions between traditions cannot be made on some 'tradition-transcendent grounds'. Yet it is possible that one of these traditions is the truth. This is what the Christian narrative claims to be: it is a meta-discourse which can and should embrace all human life and activity. Milbank describes this position as 'a true Christian meta-narrative realism'.[41] The confident assertion of the Christian narrative can save us from nihilism and violence. 'Such a Christian logic is not deconstructible by modern secular reason; rather, it is Christianity which exposes the non-necessity of supposing, like the Nietzscheans, that difference, non-totalization and indeterminacy of meaning necessarily imply arbitrariness and violence'.[42] So because Milbank's position is postmodern and historicist, he has protected the Christian narrative from secular objections. But because the narrative is true, he has protected himself against the criticism of nihilism.

In my judgement, Milbank's discussion has pointed to a difficulty in MacIntyre's position. MacIntyre wants to retain the belief that traditions are all in the same business of making sense of reality. For this to work, MacIntyre's 'traditioned-reason' must assume that the standards of coherence and intelligibility cross all traditions. (This is a point to which we shall return at the end of this chapter.) However, Milbank's alternative is equally problematic. There are two difficulties. First, it is odd to affirm the Christian narrative as a meta-discourse and yet with equal tenacity deny any legitimate rational engagement between traditions. For Milbank believes that one is not persuaded by good reasons from one tradition to another; one cannot have dialogue between traditions in a quest for the truth; and one cannot know that one's tradition describes reality in a 'more complete' way than any of the alternatives. All one can do is 'convert' (in a fideistic sense) and enact the narrative in one's life. Milbank makes this explicit in his essay in *Christian Uniqueness Reconsidered*, where he offers the following proposal for Christian relations with other religions:

> As regards the general furtherance of the critical understanding of discourses (the minimum that religions can truly share in common) it will be better to replace 'dialogue' with 'mutual suspicion'. As regards Christian theology and practice, we should simply pursue further the ecclesial project of securing harmony through difference and a continuous historical conversation not bound by the Socratic constraints of dialogue around a neutral common topic. In the course of such a conversation, we should indeed expect to constantly receive Christ again, from the unique spiritual responses of other cultures. But I do not pretend that this proposal means anything other than continuing the work of conversion.[43]

Now this is crucial. It is sad that a confident assertion of the Christian narrative is forced to have this dangerously intolerant social implication. Our tormented and divided world has more than enough 'mutual suspicion'. The Milbank outlook feeds the tribal instinct to which large parts of the Christian narrative are so strongly opposed.

The second difficulty is that Milbank's historicist assumptions undermine the possibility of writing an accurate history. Sometimes he remembers these assumptions. For example, when criticizing Wayne Meeks, he explains that one cannot get to a 'pre-textual genesis'.[44] But sometimes he forgets. Thus when he criticizes the liberal Protestant metanarrative as it initially appeared in Weber, he works through the main components, concluding: 'Hence Weber was simply wrong to discover in ancient Judaism the germs of a "protestant" religion';[45] and later 'there is no reason to suppose any identifiable Christianity before the emergence of strong ecclesial themes';[46] and once again, 'it is not true that before the Pope's assumption of imperial powers, the Church was an essentially "spiritual" body of individuals'.[47] For Milbank, Weber was wrong. No reason is given, his ideas are simply not true. This language implies strongly that the historical judgements of Weber are less appropriate than the historical judgements of Milbank. This language can only be used if one accepts that there is an objective history which can be described in better or worse ways.

Gerard Loughlin has come to the defence of Milbank. Loughlin feels that the capacity to write history involves the same conceptual difficulties as translation. He suggests that Milbank solves this problem by suggesting that we can live in several subjective worlds of discourse simultaneously.[48]

This is the point at which I must now clarify my own position. To do so, we need to root this debate about truth in the debate about realism. The task is to defend a concept of truth that takes seriously the historicist agenda. Briefly, I shall now outline the main shape of the argument that will take us into the next chapter. With Devitt, we start with the realist claim that 'objects exist independently of our minds'. The ambiguity of many anti-realists on this point is noted. The problem often is that the sorts of arguments offered by anti-realists could easily extend to idealism or solipsism. However, against Devitt, realism means nothing unless we tackle the epistemological questions.

At this point I attempt to construct arguments to underpin the possibility of a 'tradition-constituted' enquiry. 'Tradition-constituted enquiry' depends upon a critically realist account of truth. It necessarily involves the possibility of communication and, especially, communication between traditions that disagree. The writing of history depends on these conditions. Communication in turn depends on two factors; the first is translation; and the second is logic. This will take us to the end of Chapter 3.

In Chapter 4 we seek an explanation for these factors which make truth possible. The next step is to link my argument with other arguments for truth, ranging from St Augustine to Brian Hebblethwaite. By making use of St Thomas's Third Way, I intend to show that the factors underpinning truth require the existence of God.

Notes

1. Mainstream philosophy is a reference to the approach taken in the Anglo-American tradition.
2. See for example, John Hospers, *An Introduction to Philosophical Analysis* (London: Routledge, 1990) 3rd edition, pp. 182–8. Hospers confines his discussion to the big three, namely, correspondence, coherence and pragmatist. Vincent Brümmer, in *Theology and Philosophical Inquiry* (Basingstoke: Macmillan, 1981), pp. 169–78, treats the four options outlined in the text. I am not proposing to treat two further alternatives: first, the view of G. E. Moore that truth is an indefinable, inexplicable quality that some statements have and others do not. It has not attracted widespread support: and the problems with the account are manifest. Moore explains the position and identifies some of the difficulties in *Some Main Problems in Philosophy* (London: Allen & Unwin, 1953), pp. 259–63. Second, Tarski's so-called semantic theory of truth. Tarski's views are rather hard to interpret. Karl Popper, for example, considers him a straight-forward advocate of the correspondence theory, while Yourgrau

thinks this is entirely wrong. For Popper, see his 'A Realist View of Logic, Physics, and History', in *Physics, Logic and History*, edited by W. Yourgrau and A. Breck, (New York, London: Plenum Press, 1970), pp. 20f., and Yourgrau's responses in the same volume, p. 32.

3. Among contemporary defenders of correspondence, the disagreement hinges on precisely this issue. How do we bridge the gap between sentences and entities which are represented by sentences? This debate in practice concentrates on the understanding of reference. Devitt, for example, insists on a naturalistic – causal – relation. See Michael Devitt, *Realism and Truth* (Princeton: Princeton University Press, 1984), pp. 27–8.

4. The idealists found this view attractive. See for example, F. H. Bradley, *Essays on Truth and Reality* (Oxford: Clarendon Press, 1914).

5. Some might want to quarrel with this interpretation of pragmatism as an extension of coherence. This is partly because William James is unclear as to whether pragmatism offers a criterion of truth or a definition. This is linked to the related issue of whether pragmatism is meant to fit all beliefs or some only; Peirce probably intended it as a view about the establishment of scientific hypotheses, while James wanted to extend it to religious belief. My interpretation suggests that pragmatism is best seen as a supplement to the coherence theory.

6. See Richard Rorty for the most eloquent defence of this view. See R. Rorty, *Consequences of Pragmatism* (Minnesota: Minnesota University Press, 1982). Susan Haack thinks that the pragmatic theory is an attempt to combine the correspondence with the coherence. It is true that the pragmatic theory is interested in how things 'work' and therefore in that sense it has a similarity with the correspondence. However, Rorty, for example, would not want that parallel overworked. For Haack see her excellent *Philosophy of Logics* (Cambridge: Cambridge University Press, 1978), chapter 7.

7. For an excellent defence of this view, see Paul Horwich, *Truth* (Oxford: Basil Blackwell, 1990). For my purposes, his account is insufficient. Truth is a control on error: the minimalist account fails to show in what sense this is the case.

8. See A. MacIntyre, *A Short History of Ethics* (New York: Macmillan, 1966). It is worth noting that MacIntyre was not the first to make this point. Elizabeth Anscombe made the same point in

her 'Modern moral philosophy' *Philosophy*, 33 (1958). John Haldane makes the links explicit in his thoughtful critique of MacIntyre. For John Haldane see, 'MacIntyre's Thomist Revival: What Next?' in John Horton and Susan Mendus (eds.), *After MacIntyre* (Cambridge: Polity Press, 1994), pp. 92–4.

9. For Plato see the *Sophist* translated by Nicholas White (Indianapolis: Hackett Publishing Co., 1993), 240D–260C, pp. 29–54; and for Aristotle see *Categories* 15–20.

10. For example, see Augustine's discussion of truth in *The Problem of Free Choice*, translated by Mark Pontifex (London: Longmans, 1955), pp. 93f.

11. Descartes writes, 'Reason now leads me to think that I should hold back my assent from opinions which are not completely certain and indubitable just as carefully as I do from those which are patently false.' Quoted from Descartes, 'Meditations on First Philosophy' found in *The Philosophical Writings of Descartes*, translated by John Cottingham, Robert Stoothoff, and Dugald Murdock II (Cambridge: Cambridge University Press, 1984), p. 12.

12. David Hume, *A Treatise of Human Nature*, edited by L. A. Selby-Bigge, 2nd edition (Oxford: Clarendon Press, 1978), Book 1. Anthony Flew helpfully brings out the way in which Cartesian assumptions inevitably created Hume's scepticism. See A. Flew, *David Hume. Philosopher of Moral Science* (Oxford: Basil Blackwell, 1986) pp. 14–16 and pp. 109–21.

13. Henry Alison has been the main opponent of the traditional Strawson interpretation. See *Kant's Transcendental Idealism. An Interpretation and Defence* (New Haven: Yale University Press, 1983).

14. See M. Devitt, *Realism and Truth.* Devitt defines the concept of weak realism on p. 22 and links Kant with this position on pp. 59–61. As I shall discuss later, the concept of realism is apt to be confusing. Devitt's definition of 'weak realism' is simply: 'something objectively existing independently of the mental' (p. 22).

15. See William James, *Pragmatism: a new name for some old ways of thinking [and] The meaning of truth: a sequel to 'Pragmatism'* (Cambridge, Mass: Harvard University Press, 1978).

16. Peter Winch, *The Idea of a Social Science* (London: Routledge & Kegan, 1958).

17. Bryan Wilson (ed.), *Rationality* (Oxford: Basil Blackwell, 1970).

18. Wittgenstein did not in actual fact talk much about religion. However, his followers have drawn this conclusion from his work. Along with Peter Winch see D. Z. Phillips, *Faith after Foundationalism* (London: Routledge, 1988).

19. See MacIntyre in B. Wilson (ed.), *Rationality* (Oxford: Basil Blackwell, 1970), p. 68.

20. Winch in B. Wilson, ibid., p. 109.

21. Ibid., p. 109.

22. P. Winch, *The Idea of a Social Science* (London: Routledge & Kegan, 1958), pp. 100–1.

23 See for example Dennis Nineham, *The Use and Abuse of the Bible* (London: Macmillan, 1976).

24. For a good introduction to Rorty's work, see K. Kolenda, *Philosophy Democratised* (Florida: University of South Florida Press, 1990).

25. A. MacIntyre in B. Wilson, *Rationality,* p. 66.

26. Ibid., pp. 79f.

27. Ibid., p. 129.

28. Ibid., p. 129.

29. A. MacIntyre, *Whose Justice? Which Rationality?* (London: Duckworth, 1988), p. 352.

30. Ibid., p. 389.

31. Ibid., p. 355.

32. Ibid., p. 361.

33. Ibid., p. 362.

34. Ibid., p. 356.

35. Ibid., p. 365.

36. I am grateful for the insights of Robert Stern's article 'MacIntyre and Historicism' in John Horton and Susan Mendus (eds.), *After MacIntyre* (Cambridge: Polity Press, 1994), pp. 146–60.

37. John Haldane also suggests that it is not clear that MacIntyre really has escaped the relativist trap. See John Haldane, 'MacIntyre's Thomist Revival: What Next?' in John Horton and Susan Mendus (eds.), *After MacIntyre* (Cambridge: Polity Press, 1994), pp. 98–9.

38. J. Milbank, *Theology and Social Theory* (Oxford: Basil Blackwell, 1990), p. 330.

39. Ibid., pp. 341f. At this point Milbank makes certain interesting observations on the nature of translation.

40. Ibid., pp. 346–7.

41. J. Milbank, *Theology and Social Theory*, p. 389.

42. Ibid., p. 5.

43. J. Milbank in G. D'Costa (ed.), *Christian Uniqueness Reconsidered* (Maryknoll: Orbis Books 1990), p. 190.
44. J. Milbank, *Theology and Social Theory*, p. 114.
45. Ibid., p. 94.
46. Ibid., p. 94.
47. Ibid., p. 95.
48. This is a legitimate extrapolation from Loughlin's remarks. In a very good review article of Milbank's book, Loughlin criticizes me in the following way: 'Ian Markham suggests that for Milbank one cannot reject the "secular narrative" on the grounds that it is "destructive" without appealing to a "tradition-transcendent rationality". But I think this is to forget that for Milbank one can compare one narrative with another, and find one preferable to another, without recourse to a third arbitrating narrative. To use Milbank's analogy; in order to speak two languages one does not need a third which carries out a movement of equivalence or translation between the other two, nor does one need to suppose one language the equivalent of the other. One simply speaks one language and another language . . . However one accounts for the fact that people do change their stories, one does not have to suppose that they do so by measuring them against some standard (call it "reality") which, after all, can only be another story.' See Gerard Loughlin, 'Christianity at the end of the story or the return of the master-narrative', in *Modern Theology*, 8 (4) (October 1992), p. 384 note 42. Loughlin is discussing my review of Milbank's book found in *First Things*, 19 (1992): 46–8.

CHAPTER 3

Truth, language and anti-realism

In the last chapter the philosophers were chided for their lack of historical sensitivity. In this chapter many historicist 'philosophers' (like Cupitt, Rorty, and Milbank) will be chided for their lack of philosophical clarity. Two issues dominate the chapter: a) whether reality really transcends language constructs, and b) the nature of logic. I shall attempt to show that critical realism is entailed within their historicist assumptions about the community-orientated nature of knowledge. We start our discussion with the issue of realism.

Devitt and Trigg are two writers who seek to disentangle realism from epistemology.[1] For Devitt, it is his second guiding maxim for his entire evaluation of the issues relating to truth and realism. He writes: 'Maxim 2 Distinguish the metaphysical (ontological) issue of realism from any semantic issue'.[2] Devitt is right to complain that much discussion of realism has concentrated on the following issue: how can we know (or even what would it mean to know) about objects external to our minds? We have lost sight of the metaphysical question: are there any objects external to our minds? If we put the realist horse back in front of the epistemic and semantic carts (to use an image from Devitt) then many other questions would fall into place.

At this point Rorty complains that this is relatively un-interesting. He writes,

> Actually, however, this clamour about 'idealism' is a red herring.
> It is one thing to say (absurdly) that we make objects by using

words and something quite different to say that we do not know how to find a way of describing an enduring matrix of past and future inquiry into nature except in our own terms – thereby begging the question against 'alternative conceptual schemes'. Almost no one wishes to say the former. To say the latter is, when disjoined from scary rhetoric about 'losing touch with the world', just a way of saying that our present views about nature are our only guide in talking about the relations between nature and our words . . .[3]

Rorty it seems does believe in objects. However, the problem is that so many of his arguments point in the opposite direction. Cupitt also is frustrating. Sometimes he writes that 'reality' cannot transcend personal language constructs; and at other times he seems to simply assume that solipsism is absurd. So, for example, he writes, 'The surface play of phenomena – words, signs, meanings, appearances – is reality. Why seek to downgrade it? The fatal illusion is to believe that we can pierce the veil and find more real and unchanging verities behind it.'[4] Linguistic constructions of the world 'are reality'. It sounds fairly close to a form of idealism. However, when explicitly discussing idealism, Cupitt arrives at Berkeley's problem of other minds. Cupitt then dodges all the difficulties by writing: 'But we need not go into more detail: everyone knows by now that any philosophy that starts within the sphere of individual subjectivity has problems getting out into language, society and the external world.'[5] So here Cupitt is assuming the existence of the external world. Cupitt slips between insisting that the actual external world is irrelevant to the purposes of language and conceding its reality as an assumption of language. If Cupitt and Rorty find the view that words create objects 'absurd', then perhaps absurdity might take us a great deal further than they do in eliminating other views! However, before moving on too rapidly, can we provide any arguments for the external world? How precisely can we be confident that objects exist? How do we evade the Cartesian arguments for scepticism? The move most of us would accept is this: we cannot actually argue our way out of Cartesian scepticism, but we are not obliged to accept it either.[6] We can reject the sceptical puzzle altogether. Any doubts about whether we are dreaming are less than the certainty we have about the existence of tables, chairs, and doors. We are entitled to offset the lesser doubts with the greater certainties. In practice we all have to. Even if I – philosophically – doubt the existence of the door, I still have to open it upon departure.

This defence of realism – at this stage defined as 'the existence of objects not dependent on mind' – has drawn attention to the slippery tendency of opponents (i.e. of realism) to concede, or half-concede, that despite their interpretative doubts, they still believe in a world of objects. Further, their tendency is to offer arguments for an epistemological problem, which in fact would also undermine the metaphysical claim.

Nevertheless, unlike Devitt, I think realists must go further.[8] There is little benefit in affirming the existence of objects if we cannot explicate the ways in which we can distinguish between true and false descriptions of these objects. So I am defending 'critical realism', of a kind that involves three related claims:

1. World perspectives are attempts to make sense of reality as experienced.
2. Reality is the ultimate control on the legitimacy of truth claims.
3. Certain world perspectives are better than the alternatives.

By 'reality', I mean the stable world external to the mind and not dependent on the mind. This stable world incorporates all 'facts'. In my judgement these facts are not only physical, but mental and spiritual.

Part of the reason why the account of realism I want to defend needs to be more complex than that of Devitt or Trigg is that the framework in which data are interpreted is a significant problem. Illness for a medieval Christian might be interpreted in terms of spiritual powers: illness for a modern doctor is interpreted in terms of physical malfunctions. 'Common sense' does not prove the case one way or the other. Ample evidence for each account could be offered by each culture.[9] Our sense of history should make us aware that the discovery of truth is no easy task. Devitt and Trigg make it sound far too easy.

With MacIntyre, I share the conviction that the community-orientated nature of knowing needs to be taken seriously. This is the anti-realist insight, which becomes the following problem. We all live in communities. Language provides the framework in which we interpret the world. So when we compare an altar in a church with a table in my dining room, the actual data hitting our senses may be very similar. However, the terminology itself leads us to treat these two objects very differently. I can eat a meal off a table, but it would be wholly inappropriate to do the same at an altar. The interpretative framework seeks to impose order on reality, not the other way round.

However, I shall show that this argument cannot even be stated without assuming a 'critical realism'. One needs to affirm my three related claims before one can accept that knowledge is community-orientated. Communities imply the existence of other minds. Even Rorty and Cupitt accept the reality of a world of objects in which we all live and communicate. These are significant concessions to realism. The very terms in which the historicist problem is posed already assume a reality in which the problem arises. What is odd about the Cupitt position is that although the external world exists, our language constructs do not have any relation to it. The weakness here is that Cupitt is unable to offer an adequate account of translation.

Communication between two people will always involve a degree of translation. Understanding our past, our histories, will involve understanding the other. As the early MacIntyre noted against Winch, a denial of any sort of shared reality would make communication and translation impossible.

The problem of translation has generated a significant literature, much of it evolving from the work of Quine. Quine argued that the interrelated web of language (holism) means that translation is by no means easy. In *Word and Object*, Quine argues that there is no easy way of accessing reality. The first difficulty is that sentences are to be identified not with 'reality' but with sensory stimulations.[10] This is necessary because we must eliminate possible errors in perception. Then the second difficulty is that words can organize sensory stimulation in different ways. These difficulties mean that when we come to radical translation (i.e. 'translation of a language of a hitherto untouched people'),[11] we confront the principle of indeterminacy of translation.

This is best understood through the widely discussed problem of Quine's rabbit. A translator and a native are both looking at a rabbit. The native offers the word 'Gavagai', thereby implying that the word 'Gavagai' is a translation for the word 'rabbit'. Quine then writes:

> This, however, is a mistake. Stimulus synonymy of the occasion sentences 'Gavagai' and 'Rabbit' does not even guarantee that 'gavagai' and 'rabbit' are coextensive terms, terms true of the same things. For consider 'gavagai'. Who knows but what the objects to which this term applies are not rabbits after all, but mere stages, or brief temporal segments, of rabbits? In either event the stimulus situations that prompt assent to 'Gavagai' would be the same as for 'Rabbit'. Or perhaps the objects to which 'gavagai' applies are all and sundry undetached parts of rabbits; again the stimulus meaning would register no difference. When from the sameness of stimulus meanings of 'Gavagai' and 'Rabbit' the linguist leaps to the conclusion that a gavagai is a whole enduring rabbit, he is just taking for granted that the native is enough like us to have a brief general term for rabbits and no brief general term for rabbit stages or parts . . . Does it seem that the imagined indecision between rabbits, stages of rabbits, integral parts of rabbits, the rabbit fusion, and rabbithood must be due merely to some special fault in our formulation of stimulus meaning, and that it should be resoluble by a little supplementary pointing and questioning? Consider, then, how: Point to a rabbit and you have pointed to a stage of a rabbit, to an integral part of a rabbit, to the rabbit fusion, and to where rabbithood is manifested. Point to an integral part of a rabbit and you have pointed again to the remaining four sorts of things; and so on around.[12]

The point Quine is making is what he calls the principle of indeterminacy of translation.

The rabbit illustration is interesting. I have two comments. First, I am not entirely certain what all these alternatives mean.

It is difficult to know exactly what the difference is between 'rabbithood' and 'rabbit fusion'. Nor am I convinced that clarification cannot be sought by a careful study of the vocabulary surrounding this experience. Granted this would not be done by pointing; instead it might require many years of living within the culture so that the distinction might emerge. Most of us would have to spend some considerable time with Quine before we understood the difference between 'rabbithood' and 'rabbit fusion'. But presumably, Quine believes that he can explain the difference to us. And if Quine can explain in English the differences between these alternatives, by using words which have a primary meaning elsewhere, like 'hood' and 'fusion', then presumably the native would have a similar range of distinctions and be able to do the same. So if Quine is right and the native has a particularly nuanced (from our perspective) meaning for rabbit data, then it is probable (although not certain) that clues from language use elsewhere would illuminate this meaning. Secondly, and more importantly, Quine would agree that the rabbit part of experience has been successfully distinguished from a tree. 'Gavagai' is clearly something to do with rabbits. The translation is in part successful. As Trigg rightly observes:

> Exactly the same set of circumstances would always make our statement, 'There's a rabbit' and the native's 'Gavagai' true, and so there is no bar to our understanding him or his understanding us. We know what circumstances hold when he says 'Gavagai' and he could learn what circumstances hold when we say 'Rabbit' . . . The alleged indeterminacy of translation is irrelevant to whether it is logically possible to get to grips with another society's conception of the world.[13]

It seems that all Quine has spotted is that sometimes translation is approximate. Indeed certain terms are untranslatable because there is no corresponding space in the other language to embrace the concept. This every translator knows is true. MacIntyre has a linked anxiety when he returns to the issue of translation in *Whose Justice? Which Rationality?* This time his treatment of translation involves a different problem. Earlier, MacIntyre's concern had been with Winch's belief that the total otherness of cultures renders understanding impossible. Here, by contrast, his concern is the complacent way in which liberals, using an international language, imagine that everything can be effortlessly translated.[14] He emphasizes the considerable (and sometimes insurmountable) difficulties involved in translation. For MacIntyre, there are numerous languages. Even a given nation has different languages-in-use for different communities, and the English of the sixteenth century was not the same as that today.[15] Further, translation of a particular text will not include all the explanatory beliefs that make the text fully intelligible.[16] This means that when two traditions meet there will be certain concepts that are untranslatable. Understanding will only come through learning a second first language (i.e. becoming bilingual so that the second language is known as intimately as the first). A person thus equipped will understand the explanatory purpose of the language from within.

So MacIntyre believes that modernity must confront the difficulties involved in translation. This confrontation will be difficult for modernity: 'The thought which modernity, whether conservative or radical, rejects is that there may be traditional modes of social, cultural, and intellectual life which are as such inaccessible to it and to its translators.'[17] And, against those who insist that 'inaccessible' parts of a different language depend on understanding, MacIntyre writes:

> But if it is in the case, as I have argued here, that a condition of discovering the inaccessible is in fact a matter of two stages, in the first of which we acquire a second language-in-use as a second first language and only in the second of which can we learn that we are unable to translate what we are now able to say in our second first language into our first first language, then this argument loses all its force.[18]

So MacIntyre arrives at the odd position that although translation is impossible, it is possible to understand that which is untranslatable.

In many respects I prefer the clarity of the earlier MacIntyre. In his later work he is in danger of undermining his more general case. If one shares the community-orientated emphasis of MacIntyre, then the possibility of community does depend on communication. Further if MacIntyre is right to insist that there are many 'languages-in-use' with variations from generation to generation, then problems of communication emerge even within a tradition. However, communication depends on understanding and translation. We may grant that translation can be difficult, and that certain concepts will be untranslatable. But because our experiences of the world are the same (at least in the sense that we all encounter stones, cats, and tables), there is also a high degree of hopefulness. Further as Stephen Fowl has shown, MacIntyre's requirements for understanding another culture would make, for example, the study of ancient Greek religion virtually impossible.[19] It is very difficult to become so acquainted with that culture that one knows it as intimately as our own. And MacIntyre must see this because vast sections of his work are devoted to providing a historical account of very different cultures and traditions.

It is my contention that communication and related activities involved in communication, such as translation, are only intelligible if one assumes that language constructs emerge as an attempt to explain reality. Attempts to explain translation without recourse to this assumption fail. We have seen that the early MacIntyre would have agreed; the later MacIntyre is less clear. It is now necessary to return to John Milbank and Gerard Loughlin. They attempt to move in the opposite direction. However, as we will now see, Milbank's position is very problematic.

Milbank seems to share my awkwardness in even understanding MacIntyre. But where I have argued that MacIntyre needs critical realism, Milbank stresses incommensurability. His position can be outlined in four points:

1. Radical disagreement must assume some background agreement. I cannot disagree with something that I cannot understand at all. This would create complete incomprehension.

2. However, there is a significant disagreement between an insider's and an outsider's knowledge. The latter only entertains beliefs, the former is completely committed.

3. We do not entertain alternative ideas to our own by finding equivalents in one language for ideas in the other.

4. Instead we engage the other by holding 'inside our heads several subjectivities, even if some of these are merely entertained'.[20] So when Milbank is in America, he does not find English equivalents for American, but instead, 'I simply become American *as well as* English, or more American for a time, before reverting'.[21]

Milbank believes that he can hold several different languages in his head simultaneously without making any links. The reason why he does not want to make any links is because a link might imply an external reality which in some sense is a control on our language. And this is his mistake. The purpose of language is to explicate reality: and translation can only happen if this is assumed. This can be illustrated by examining his English–American linguistic gap.

The American–English example is of course not as difficult as Quine's 'radical translation'. I concede that translation difficulties do arise here, although, I note in passing, these are often no greater than a gap between parents and children. However, consider the following translation difficulty: an Oxford don uses the euphemism 'may I wash my hands?' when asking for the toilet.[22] He meets an American who prefers the term 'rest room'. Now there is potential for misunderstanding here: the don might show the American to the bedroom, while the American might point to the kitchen taps. Fairly rapidly both would discover that their respective euphemisms mean the same and refer to an object in reality known in my culture as the toilet. Now I suspect that the don would decide that 'rest room' is the American equivalent for 'may I wash my hands': and he certainly would expect external reality (i.e. the bedroom or the kitchen would be wrong) to control the actual meaning.

It is worth at this point pausing to see how this illustration requires the three critically realist claims. First, both English and American cultures need a statement that expresses the need for the toilet. The activity is a part of reality and this needs linguistic expressions. This illustrates my first claim, namely, that world perspectives are attempts to make sense of reality. Second, both cultures would allow the object in reality to determine the legitimacy of the translation. This illustrates my second claim, namely, that reality is the ultimate control on the legitimacy of truth claims. The third only arises when cultures disagree. Translation can also illustrate this. An Eskimo insists that there are many different types of snow, and an English person disagrees by insisting that it is all just 'snow'. This disagreement is best resolved by reality. Presumably the English person could, perhaps after a little training, see the fine distinctions for which the Eskimo has particular words. If so, then when it comes to 'snow' the Eskimo has the better and more refined world-perspective.

Returning then to Milbank. He finds himself forced to such an odd (and extremely implausible) account of translation because of a fear of admitting an external world making any sort of difference. He concludes his discussion against MacIntyre by writing:

> Only philosophic realism, he [i.e. MacIntyre] contends, which does not confuse its own present outlook with the way things really are, will be open to other ways of looking at things. No doubt this sounds seductive for the many 'critical realist' theologians of our times, but it assumes, first, that different cultural discourses are approximations to the same external (even if not independently specifiable) reality, and, second, that our openness to the recognition of cultural difference keeps pace with our acknowledgment of new dimensions of 'reality'.[23]

Milbank is right that MacIntyre's view does depend on world perspectives all interpreting the same external world. And I have shown that all translation must make that assumption. To translate from one language to another, we have to assume that the purpose of language is to make sense of reality. The data 'rabbit' and 'toilet' exist in the external world; and the external world determines the appropriate equivalent. Further, if we assume that American and English are different languages, and that their 'differences' are no greater than those between generations, then one rapidly approaches the thought that every person has (to a degree but in principle) a different language. And if this is so, then *all* communication between human beings depends on this assumption of a shared external world.

The argument thus far is this: language is 'tradition-constituted'. However, one should not move from this fact to anti-realism. For language must imply, as a bare minimum, the existence of other minds and the existence of communities. Language makes very little sense if other people do not exist. Further, communication and translation assume that the purpose of language is the construction of world perspectives that make sense of the world we share with others. We cannot translate unless we assume that the external world provides the standard to determine legitimacy.

This argument from translation to the critically realist instinct is endorsed by a further assumption underpinning language. This is the basic rules of theoretical rationality – the fundamental laws of logic. Language depends on certain rules being observed. The grammar of language is logic. Logic not only points beyond itself to critical realism, but also points to the character of the world. This does not require a 'realism' in logic; instead one is simply marvelling at the way in which logic seems to fit the world. If the rules underpinning the possibility of language are justified, then they require explanation. This will be the route of argument from truth to the existence of God. However, this is to go too quickly, we must first examine the rational assumptions underpinning all language.

Logic, language, and reality

When it comes to the translation of logical connectives, Quine insists that fair translation should preserve logical laws.[24] When a native of an alien culture seems to have offered a contradiction, the translator should search for linguistic turns that would eliminate the seeming contradiction. Consider the law of non-contradiction: we cannot envisage a language and culture that talks simultaneously of a table that is not a table. The law of non-contradiction rightly insists that nothing could be said if this were the case. That which has been affirmed, namely 'this is a table', has suddenly been denied by the negation 'this is not a table'. The net result is that nothing has been stated; the two halves have cancelled each other out.

Davidson's 'Principle of Charity', arguing at this point along lines similar to Quine, is correct at least in this respect. One must, when engaging the other, assume that the fundamentals of logic apply.[25] Yet this view nevertheless poses an interesting and difficult question. What precisely is the relation between logic, language, and reality? The argument from translation has sought to illustrate a significant link between language and reality. I have argued that the purpose of language is to 'make sense' of reality, and that it is only operating with this assumption that translation is possible. If Quine and Davidson are right, then we further see the centrality of logic in this process. Logic is linked with language and language is linked with reality. We have a triad which I want to argue support each other.

The significance of logic is partly located in its universal claim. Translators, Quine and Davidson insist, ought to concede its cross-cultural significance. The fundamental logical laws seem to be essential to the possibility of any language. We cannot imagine successful communication between people succeeding without these laws.

Peter Winch's famous challenge to this has already been quoted: 'criteria of logic are not a direct gift of God . . .'[26] This, of course, is true. As historicists repeatedly remind us, everything has a story; and logic is no exception. The story of logic runs like this: in the Western tradition, Aristotle was the first to reflect critically on the nature of arguments and identify some of the basic conditions of validity. However, even though Kant thought that Aristotle's logic was the last word, in actual fact it has proved capable of dramatic developments, especially since Kant's day.[27] Aristotle's syllogism actually proved to be but a small sub-section of predicate logic. And with the development of symbolic logic, the discipline flourished. Leibniz is normally given the credit for being 'the first serious student of symbolic logic'.[28] George Boole improved on the system, and the story moves on to Peirce in the United States and Peano in France, culminating in the calculus of Russell's *Principia Mathematica.* Of course, logic has a history, as has historicism, relativism, and everything else. But the question remains: what exactly did logic, as developed from Aristotle to Russell 'discover'? And is it universal in significance?

One difficulty in answering these questions is that this century has seen a proliferation of logics. Susan Haack lists the following formal logics:

'traditional' logic – Aristotelian syllogistic

'classical' logic – 2-valued sentence calculus
– predicate calculus

'extended' logics – modal logic
– tense logics
– deontic logics
– epistemic logics
– preference logics
– imperative logics
– erotetic (interrogative) logics

'deviant' logics – many-valued logics
– intuitionist logics
– quantum logics
– free logics

'inductive' logics[29]

The traditional, classical, and extended logics can be accommodated as a family in a single story with relative ease. Aristotle grasped certain basic forms of argument: the classical logic offered a system of basic axioms that could resolve questions about invalidity; while the extended logics simply 'extended' logic's domain to questions about time or the difference between statements using the concepts necessary and contingent. Here one has the sense of the edifice sharing the same foundations, but simply going a storey higher. Furthermore inductive logic can complement classical deductive logic. So although it is not best seen as another storey, it is a building that fits nicely alongside.

The problem logics, which have provoked some logicians into talking about a 'plurality' of logics, are the deviant ones.

Quantum logic, for example, claims that at the molecular level the law of excluded middle does not operate. The problem lies with Heisenberg's uncertainty principle, which states that one cannot measure the motion and, simultaneously, identify the location of an electron. *Prima facie* there appears to be a conflict. When one observes the electron's motion, one cannot ask for its location; and when one observes its location, one cannot ask about its motion. Putnam, for example, has argued that quantum mechanics requires a third value; a statement can be true or false or middle.[30] If this is correct, then this would undermine the universality of logic. We would now have a discourse that needs a significantly different logic.

Does the New Physics require this radical shift? Popper, for example, is adamant that it does not. He writes:

> There is, therefore, no reason whatever to accept either Heisenberg's or Bohr's subjectivist interpretation of quantum mechanics. Quantum mechanics is a statistical theory because the problems it tries to solve – spectral intensities, for example – are statistical problems. There is, therefore, no need here for any philosophical defence of its non-causal character . . . [T]here is no reason whatsoever to doubt the realist and objectivistic character of all physics.[31]

Whether or not Popper is ultimately right, he does sound a warning about accepting too readily the apparent implications of the New Physics for logic. And, anyway, the difficulty with the construction of a new logic for a branch of science which is still very recent and hard to understand is that it undermines the central features of logic for what may seem limited and borderline reasons.

Traditionally, logic has been defined as the science of the laws of thought. It is distinct from psychology because that studies how people in actual fact think, while logic examines the way people *ought* to think. It distinguishes good from bad reasoning. This traditional definition of logic is clearly true of formal logic. For formal deductive logic identifies the circumstances under which one can deduce conclusions from a set of premises. Formal deductive logic is, Popper explains, a 'transmitter of truth':

Derivability or deduction involves, essentially, the transmission of truth and the retransmission of falsity: in a valid inference truth is transmitted from the premisses to the conclusion. This can be used especially in so-called 'proofs'. But falsity is also re-transmitted from the conclusion to (at least) one of the premisses, and this is used in disproofs or refutations, and especially in critical discussions.[32]

Popper's enthusiasm for deductive logic made him very critical of inductive logic. He believed it was possible to account for scientific explanations in a deductive way. Although most logicians were not convinced, the debate exposed certain characteristics of formal deductive logic. It seems to be a condition of language; there is an indispensable air to it. However, against Popper, one needs to link deductive logic with inductive logic. Both types share certain characteristics: they are both attempting to provide rules of legitimate reasoning; both set out conditions for reaching conclusions about the world.[33] This is not making a realist claim for logic. Instead the rules of logic are embedded in language and seem to fit the world. In other words as we interpret data, so we attempt to understand them, and in understanding them we construct arguments – arguments that justify the particular understanding we find most convincing.

Because I take the laws of logic to be universal in their operation, I am opposed to instrumentalism[34] (i.e. the view that logic is simply a matter of convention and can vary for different groups). The possibility of communication across groups, cultures, generations, and even between individuals would be unintelligible if this were not the case. If the rules of inference were not shared, then discussion and under-standing would become impossible. I am also opposed to pluralism (i.e. the view that there are plural correct forms of logic). Logic makes a claim which is universal – true of all entities that can reason. Nothing, not even God, can think (i.e. reason) in a different way. Pluralism would undermine this universalism.

Therefore, although I am a monist (i.e. hold that ultimately there is one correct system of logic), this does not necessarily entail that all logical truths have already been discovered.

Unlike Kant, I do not see an incompatibility between monism and revision and discovery.

Logical truths were discovered as a necessary condition for language. They have a history. We can and shall continue to make discoveries. And it is in principle possible that we might have to modify our existing understanding of logic to accommodate these new discoveries. Haack is right when she explains her claim that logic is revisable: 'What I mean . . . is not that the truths of logic might be otherwise than they are, but that the truths of logic might be other than we take them to be, i.e. we could be mistaken about what the truths of logic are, e.g. in supposing that the law of excluded middle is one such.'[35] This means that deviant logics are important, for they can make new proposals that may lead to modification of our current understanding of logic. This account is attempting to protect logic's universal quality, crossing cultures and languages.

Logic then seems to be a universal condition for human language. It succeeds because it seems to fit the world. I think this should be a matter for amazement and surprise. We cannot operate without these laws of logic. Things are not contradictory; the weighing of evidence does often reach true conclusions about the world; and people are correctly persuaded when good arguments are provided. It is not necessary to envisage an almost Platonic realist concept of logic; instead we have a tool that is indispensable precisely because it fits the world.

Let us now link these reflections on the universal nature of logic with the argument for critical realism. The picture that is now emerging is as follows. Individuals live in community. Each person grows up within the interpretative framework of the community. As persons learn to reason, so they find elements in reality that both endorse and undermine the framework. The weight given to these elements in reality will vary considerably from community to community, but the means of weaving them together will be shared, whether applied truly or falsely. For example, a Christian community will find the order in the world more significant than the disorder, while for an atheist community it may be the other way round. The Christian is likely to give more 'weight' to the order. However, both Christian and atheist will process the material in a way that observes the fundamental requirements of logic.[36]

We have a two-way process. Facts in the world, transmitted[37] through logical processes, alter the interpretative framework; and a belief in that framework, transmitted through logical processes, is confirmed by the facts in the world. Naturally, much of this process is subconscious and very little happens in isolation. We are community animals, although sometimes a genius makes an exceptional discovery acting alone. The logical processes of deduction and induction make certain assumptions about the world. This 'transmission tunnel' between reality and mind must assume that the transmission tunnel captures the nature of the world in some way. Logic, to put it crudely, assumes that the world is not chaotic. Instead, for logic to be legitimate the world must be intelligible.

Logic is the tool by which we explain the world. Explanations are an interplay between already existing understanding (the mental framework given by and in one's community), the data in the world (reality) and logical processes. It is a logical demand that explanations offered should be coherent.

We seem to have only two options: does this coherence mirror the world or is it imposed? A Kantian type anti-realist would insist it is the latter. Or at least she would say that we cannot get beyond our mentally created 'coherent explanations' to find out what reality is really like. On this view reality might be chaotic. However, the problems with this are considerable. First, we return to the problems of solipsism and idealism. What is the extent of this chaos? Does it embrace other people who are after all simply a part of the external world? Second, the universal nature of logic seems to indicate that, while not impossible, it is unlikely. Granted it is only unlikely (we are not completely certain), all the same, as a tool of communication, language is successful. And this is good evidence, because if this success is partly due to shared cultural observance of these fundamental laws, then this would seem to imply that the public domain (in which people and objects exist) must mirror fairly closely the fundamentals of logic.

This suggests that the alternative view is preferable; this is the position of the critical realist. The logical processes are justified because they mirror the way the world is. The world is indeed coherent. It is a stable, explicable entity, which does not contradict itself. If the world were contradictory, then the logical processes would be misleading our mind. We would not be constructing a true picture of the world, because the coherence demanded by logic would be mind imposed. The point is simple: reality must be stable, coherent, and intelligible; otherwise our logical categories on which all truth claims depend are misguided.

This now enables us to return to the debate between the realist and the anti-realist. I have argued that since MacIntyre's work, the situation is significantly different. In the discussion so far there have been four main options; and in the next chapter I shall offer my own alternative (see chart 1).

CHART 1			
Critical Realism		**Anti-Realism**	
Position 1	*Position 2*	*Position 3*	*Position 4*
Realism	Critical Realist Historicism	Theological Realist Historicism	Anti-Realism
Michael Devitt	Alasdair MacIntyre	John Milbank	Don Cupitt

The first of the four is realism, represented and defended by Michael Devitt.[38] He links his realism to the correspondence theory of truth and affirms the existence of common sense objects and scientific objects. Brian Hebblethwaite also identifies with this position, although he adds to the range of objects in reality.[39] At the opposite end of the spectrum, the fourth position, we find Don Cupitt.[40] Although he does in fact believe in the external world (and, therefore, like Kant is a weak realist), he believes it is irrelevant and inaccessible. We must make do with language signs. These signs cannot be transcended.

In between, in position two, on the critical-realist side of the spectrum, we have Alasdair MacIntyre.[41] He is committed to historicism, but explains development and change in traditions by reference to their explanatory power which is determined by reality. Position three is on the anti-realist side. John Milbank is historicist yet a theological realist.[42] We cannot discover which tradition explains the world best, but certain metanarratives might simply be true.

Milbank's strongest point against MacIntyre is that the comparison of traditions in terms of explanatory power must involve a 'tradition-transcendent' set of criteria. Unlike Milbank, I think these criteria are partly provided by the universal logical processes that are shared across culture. However, these logical processes assume the existence of an external world which itself is stable, coherent, and intelligible. This assumption about the world requires explanation. However, as Aquinas demonstrated in formulating the cosmological argument, this explanation cannot be contingent.

Notes

1. Michael Devitt makes this point at some length, see *Realism and Truth*, chapter 4. Roger Trigg defines realism as 'a thesis about the status of real entities, and not about our knowledge of them'. See *Reality at Risk. A Defence of Realism in Philosophy and the Sciences* (New York: Harvester Wheatsheaf, 1989), p. xix.
2. Michael Devitt, *Realism and Truth*, p. 3.
3. Richard Rorty, *Philosophy and the Mirror of Nature* (Oxford: Basil Blackwell, 1980), p. 276.
4. Don Cupitt, *The Long-Legged Fly* (London: SCM Press, 1987), p. 20. Scott Cowdell in his excellent study of Don Cupitt's writings makes a very pertinent point on Cupitt's 'complete constructivism' found in *The Long-Legged Fly*: 'A genuine act of faith is called for to believe that nothing exists outside the mind.' Quite so! See Scott Cowdell, *Atheist Priest? Don Cupitt and Christianity* (London: SCM Press, 1988), pp. 61–2.
5. Don Cupitt, *Creation out of Nothing* (London: SCM Press, 1990), p. 48. In a strange way, Cupitt is endorsing my case. However, the difference between us is that once he concedes the necessary

assumptions essential for his language-constituted reality, then I think these assumptions entitle us to go a great deal further.

6. See Devitt who takes this line in *Realism and Truth*, pp. 51–2.

7. It is worth noting that even Rorty and Cupitt (in certain moods) can affirm this concept of realism.

8. To give Devitt his due, while in principle he believes that it is important to separate the issues, in fact he does go further by then linking his realism with a correspondence theory of truth.

9. Dennis Nineham makes much of this problem in his *The Use and the Abuse of the Bible* (London: Macmillan, 1976).

10. W. V. O. Quine, *Word and Object* (Cambridge, Mass: MIT Press, 1960), pp. 30–1.

11. Ibid., p. 28.

12. Ibid., pp. 51–3.

13. R. Trigg, *Reason and Commitment* (Cambridge: Cambridge University Press, 1973), p. 158.

14. MacIntyre makes this point in *Whose Justice? Which Rationality?*, p. 385.

15. Ibid., p. 373.

16. Ibid., p. 384.

17. Ibid., p. 387.

18. Ibid., p. 387.

19. See Stephen Fowl, 'Could Horace Talk with the Hebrews? Translatability and Moral Disagreement in MacIntyre and Stout', in *Journal of Religious Ethics*, 19 (1) (Spring 1991): 1–20.

20. John Milbank, *Theology and Social Theory*, p. 341.

21. Ibid., p. 341.

22. It is difficult to think of an appropriate illustration of the linguistic gap between the English and the Americans. One of the problems with the illustration offered is that almost all the terms are euphemisms, including toilet and lavatory. However, despite this limitation, the illustration is only intending to make the point that the external world is a determining factor in legitimate translation.

23. Ibid., pp. 343–4.

24. Quine, *Word and Object*, p. 59.

25. For a helpful discussion see Simon Evnine, *Donald Davidson* (Stanford: Stanford University Press, 1991), pp. 101–5. In my judgement, Davidson is correct when it comes to logic, but the principle might become problematic if one extends it too far. I do think that an entire culture might be significantly mistaken.

26. P. Winch, *The Idea of a Social Science* (London: Routledge & Kegan, 1958), pp. 100–1. See back to chapter 8, note 32.

27. Kant writes, 'Logic, by the way, has not gained much in content since Aristotle's times and indeed it cannot, due to its nature. But it may well gain in exactness, definiteness, and distinctiveness. There are but few sciences that can come into a permanent state beyond which they undergo no further change. To these belong logic, and also metaphysics. Aristotle had omitted no moment of the understanding; we are herein only more exact, methodological, and orderly'. Immanuel Kant, *Logic*, translated by R. Hartman and W. Schwarz (New York: The Bobbs-Merrill Company, 1974), p. 23.

28. C. Lewis and C. Langford, 'The Development of Symbolic Logic' in I. Copi and J. Gould in *Contemporary Readings in Logical Theory* (New York: Macmillan, 1967), p. 5.

29. Susan Haack, *Philosophy of Logics* (Cambridge: Cambridge University Press, 1978), p. 4. Much of this discussion on logic is heavily dependent on her excellent treatment of these issues in this book.

30. H. Putnam, 'Three-Valued Logic' in *Philosophical Studies*, 8 (5) (October 1957): 73–80.

31. Karl Popper, 'A Realist View of Logic, Physics, and History', in *Physics, Logic and History*, edited by W. Yourgrau and A. Breck (New York/London: Plenum Press, 1970), p. 17.

32. Ibid., p. 18.

33. The difference between deductive and inductive logic has created the problem. With deductive arguments if an argument is valid and the premises true, then the conclusion must be true. With an inductive argument it is possible to have a valid form and true premises, but a false conclusion. However, this difference should not overlook the significant similarities.

34. Susan Haack has provided this terminology. See, *Philosophy of Logics*, chapter 12.

35. Ibid., p. 232.

36. So MacIntyre is right to talk of different rationalities, if by that he means the weight given to certain factors, rather than the logical fundamentals that process those factors. See *Whose Justice? Which Rationality?*

37. 'Transmitted' should not be confused with the sense already seen in the work of Karl Popper. I simply mean that interpretation of the world uses the logical processes.

38. See M. Devitt, *Realism and Truth*.

39. See B. Hebblethwaite, *The Ocean of Truth.*
40. See D. Cupitt, *Creation out of Nothing.*
41. See A. MacIntyre, *Whose Justice? Which Rationality?*
42. See J. Milbank, *Theology and Social Theory.*

CHAPTER 4

The argument from truth to God

Alasdair MacIntyre has played a very significant role in the argument thus far, and this chapter will be no exception. We have seen in Chapter 2 how MacIntyre, in his discussion with Winch, identifies the main difficulties with anti-realism. We then used some of his arguments in *Whose Justice? Which Rationality?* to formulate an argument from 'language assumptions' (i.e. the conditions necessary to enable communication) to critical realism. However, with Milbank and against MacIntyre, I argued that critical realism does assume a shared rationality which is able to provide the framework for comparison between competing traditions. The shared rationality is found in our logical categories that must in some sense mirror the world. The world must be coherent; otherwise language would not be able to describe the world. In this chapter I shall develop MacIntyre's argument that St Thomas is 'tradition-constituted', and what this implies for natural theology. Then I shall stand in this *tradition* of natural theology and defend the claim that the possibility of truth depends on belief in God.

Most people in our culture would find such a claim fantastic. Despite a grand ancestry for the argument from truth to God (from Augustine, Anselm, to Brian Hebblethwaite), it meets strong resistance.[1] This is partly due to its implications. For example, atheists who claim that the truth is that there is no God become incoherent. If truth implies the existence of God, then one cannot believe in truth and the non-existence of God. But it is also partly due to a basic confusion. As we saw in Chapter 1, the confusion arises because it is difficult to see why a belief about the origin of the universe should make any difference to the possibility of truth in general. Popular Western culture treats the question of God's existence on the same level as questions about other mysterious entities: there might be a Loch Ness Monster; other creatures might live in outer space; and there might be this alarmingly large entity called God who started the entire universe.

This is the reason why I offered an alternative account of what being religious involves. I suggested that the claim that there is a God is a part of an all-embracing world perspective – one which sees the universe as ultimately personal rather than impersonal. One that sees morality as a matter of dis- covery rather than invention. And one that grounds the possibility of truth in the reality of God. So on this view it is not simply a contingency of history that relativism in morality and truth has run parallel with the rise of secularism. Instead they are logically connected.

I shall now examine three arguments from truth to God: two are ancient (Augustine and Anselm), and one contem- porary (Brian Hebblethwaite). All three differ significantly from the argument I am constructing, while offering certain points of comparison and confirmation.

Arguments from truth to God

Augustine's natural theology is often neglected. Even though Etienne Gilson described it as 'perhaps, the most profound and most constant element in his metaphysical thought',[2] it has not received much attention. Certainly, it is central to his theodicy. As Geivett has pointed out, if one is certain that God exists, then the problem of evil is much less of a problem.[3] The argument from truth to God is given prominent treat- ment in *On the Free Choice of the Will.* Here Augustine's sparring partner is Evodius.

The argument starts from the certainty that each person exists in a world of animals, stones, and stars.[4] Further there are different levels of existence: stones just exist, animals have life but not consciousness, and humans have life and consciousness. Consciousness is defined in terms of reason or, more precisely, the 'inner sense' that organizes and interprets life. Augustine then argues that if something higher than humans could be established, this would be God. Evodius rightly objects that there might be something greater than reason but still not as great as God. Augustine in reply takes the following line:

> Then it will be enough for me to show that something of this sort exists, which you can admit to be God; or if something yet higher exists you will concede that is God. Therefore, whether there is something higher or not, it will be manifest that God exists, when I with his help fulfill my promise to prove that there is something higher than reason.[5]

This does not actually follow: one cannot exclude the possibility that there is a plethora of entities higher than human reason, none of which have the attributes we associate with God. A proof establishing the existence of at least one higher entity greater than human reason would not make God demonstrable.

However, let us grant Augustine his assumption and see how the argument develops. Augustine now moves to the possibility of truth claims. He includes claims made on the basis of sense data (to use modern terminology), and mathematical claims. He insists they point to a unity that is ultimately immutable. Individuals' interpretations do not undermine the concept of a single truth. He writes:

> Then this truth is a single truth that can be seen in common by all who know it. Nonetheless, each person sees it with his own mind – not with yours or mine or anyone else's – even though the truth that is seen is present in common to everyone who sees it.[6]

This truth is synonymous with God. He reaches the climax in a splendid eulogy:

> So you cannot deny the existence of an unchangeable truth that contains everything that is unchangeably true . . . I had promised,

if you recall, that I would prove that there is something more sublime than our mind and reason. Here it is: the truth itself. Embrace it, if you can; enjoy it; 'delight in the Lord, and he will give you the desires of your heart.' What more can you desire than happiness? And what greater happiness can there be than to enjoy the unshakable, unchangeable, and most excellent truth? . . . The truth shows forth all good things that are true, holding them to be grasped by whoever has understanding and chooses one or many of them for his enjoyment . . . This is our freedom, when we are subject to the truth; and the truth is God himself, who frees us from death, that is, from the state of sin.[7]

Commentators have reacted in two different ways. Some, like Henry Chadwick, treat it as peripheral and interpret it as a part of Augustine's Neoplatonism. Chadwick writes,

In Augustine's hands the argument about God's existence merges into the argument of the Platonists for the reality of universals as eternal and immutable truths, whether these be of mathematics or of transcendent values of justice and truth, in the light of which the mind judges whether a particular action or proposition is just or true.[8]

Certainly, Chadwick is right to see Neoplatonic assumptions about the world of the forms providing the reality that underpins all knowledge. However, the setting counts against the argument being treated as trivial. Augustine is trying to justify 'trusting God': both trusting that it was good that God gave us free will and trusting that God exists against the sincere enquiry of the sceptic. Augustine asks Evodius immediately prior to the argument:

Scripture says, 'The fool has said in his heart, "There is no God".' Suppose one of those fools were to say that to you. Suppose he did not want to believe what you believe, but to know whether what you believe is true. Would you just give up, or would you think that he could somehow be persuaded of what you firmly believe – especially if he was not merely contentious, but sincerely wanted to know?[9]

This shows clearly that Augustine does expect this argument to persuade the sceptic. And therefore it should not be treated as peripheral to his thought.

Others, such as Etienne Gilson, believe it to be central, yet treat it as mystical. It captures the stages involved in the soul's journey to God; it describes the struggle from knowledge of 'sensible things' to knowledge of God. It is, if you like, intended to be a theological version of Plato's famous 'myth of the cave'. Gilson writes, 'It is neither an argument nor a series of arguments, but a complete metaphysics plus an ethics and a mysticism which crowns it'.[10] It is true that the eulogy about truth (coupled with the sun metaphor) points to a mystical strand. However, like Chadwick, Gilson has overlooked Augustine's intention. His purpose is to construct an argument sufficient to persuade the atheist fool. We should not let Augustine's style make us ignore his stated purpose.

However odd it might sound, it seems clear that Augustine is constructing an argument that moves from any true proposition (such as our own existence) to the reality of God. He is further implying that a sceptic who is certain about his own existence should be persuaded by the argument. Augustine has an overwhelming sense of the all-embracing nature of the Christian claim. God, for Augustine, is not simply an object that might or might not exist and is irrelevant to the existence of other objects. Although the particular shape of this argument uses Neoplatonic language, which we can no longer share, it still rightly appeals to the mystery of truth as a datum that requires explanation. This, as I have already implied and will develop further later, is a legitimate requirement.

The second argument from truth to God is found in Anselm.[11] He starts his *Monologion* by acknowledging a significant debt to St Augustine.[12] Everything contained in the *Monologion*, claims Anselm, is compatible with Augustine's writings. So it is not surprising that in a meditation devoted to reflecting on the nature of God without recourse to revelation one finds Augustine's argument from truth. It comes when Anselm is discussing God and eternity in chapter eighteen:

> Moreover, if the Supreme Nature were to have a beginning or an end it would not be true eternity – something which we have already uncontestably found it to be. Or again, let anyone who

can, try to conceive of when it began to be true, or was ever not true, that something was going to exist. Or (let him try to conceive of) when it will cease being true and will not be true that something has existed in the past. Now if neither of these things can be conceived, and if both statements can be true only if there is truth, then it is impossible even to think that truth has a beginning or an end. Indeed, suppose that truth had had a beginning, or suppose that it would at some time come to an end: Then even before truth had begun to be, it would be true that there was no truth; and even after truth had come to an end, it would still be true that there would be no truth. But it could not be true without truth. Hence, there would have been truth before truth came to be, and there would still be truth after truth had ceased to be. But these conclusions are self-contradictory. Therefore, whether truth is said to have a beginning or an end, or whether it is understood not to have a beginning or end, truth cannot be confined by any beginning or end. Consequently, the same conclusion holds with regard to the Supreme Nature, because the Supreme Nature is the Supreme Truth.[13]

Anselm is proving God's eternity by arguing from truth to its eternal nature. He assumes that truth is synonymous with God. Clearly, he thought this argument incomplete, because he followed the *Monologion* with his dialogue, *De Veritate*. The pupil starts the dialogue by quoting this passage from the *Monologion*, and asks his teacher to define truth. The teacher, with some sophistication, looks at the whole range of problems associated with truth: from the difference between sentences and the objects that sentences describe to problems of perception, for example, the stick appearing bent in water. The climax is reached when the pupil discerns that truth consists in rightness. Rightness embraces truth in thoughts, truth in behaviour, and truth in perception. Now there are not many 'truths' here; rather, Anselm concludes:

> We speak improperly when we say 'the truth of this thing' or 'the truth of that thing'. For truth does not have its being in or from or through the things in which it is said to be. But when these things are in accordance with truth, which is always present to things which are as they ought to be, then we say 'the truth of this thing' or 'the truth of that thing' (for example, 'the truth of

the will' or 'the truth of action'). Similarly, we say 'the time of this thing' or 'the time of that thing', although there is one and the same time for all things which exist together at the same time. And if this thing did not exist or if that thing did not exist, time would nonetheless remain the same; for we say 'the time is in these things' but because these things are in time, we say 'the time of this thing' or 'the time of that thing'. Similarly, Supreme Truth, existing in and of itself, is not the truth of anything; but when something accords with Supreme Truth, then we speak of the truth, or rightness, of that thing.[14]

The problem in analysing Anselm's argument is that it is an indirect proof of God. We arrive at God via the eternal nature of the Supreme Truth, which is assumed to be God. *De Veritate* is intended to establish that truth is an unity, thereby justifying the identification of truth with God.

Perhaps because of the stress on eternity and unity, we can understand G. R. Evans' summary of the *Monologion*:

> In his first book, the *Monologion*, he suggests that the way to get an idea of a God who is the highest good is to climb up a ladder of goods in one's mind, beginning with the familiar good things of everyday life. A profoundly Platonic conception of the Supreme Being is thus as it were tethered to common experience and a God ultimately unknowable by human intellect is present in human terms.[15]

So for Evans, these are traditional medieval arguments for the Neoplatonic timeless God. Yet before we leave Anselm, Brian Hebblethwaite makes an interesting point: 'I am not suggesting that we discover there to be only one fundamental and all-encompassing truth.'[16] So Hebblethwaite is opposed to the idealist conviction, apparently shared by Anselm, that the Supreme Truth must be a unity. However, Hebblethwaite goes on,

> But we do discover the connectedness of things in an intelligible universe; and the supposition of a single mind and will behind the one system and its many products justifies to some extent Anselm's view expressed in *De Veritate* that in discerning the truth of how particular things are, we gain some points of access to the supreme truth of God.[17]

In making this distinction between 'unity' and 'con-
nectedness', and in affirming that truth has the latter quality
but not the former, Hebblethwaite is disentangling the
argument from its Neoplatonic roots. It is a distinctive reading of Anselm, which flies in the face of a repeated refrain
in his writing to the effect that truth is not simply inter-
connected but a single unity. However, Hebblethwaite is
correct in making this move. Truth is a property of sentences
realized when they accurately describe reality. Truth is not,
as in a Neoplatonic framework, an entity. Hebblethwaite is
attempting to reformulate this tradition in a way that is more
acceptable to our age.

So we turn to examine Hebblethwaite's own argument
in detail. He starts by using the arguments of Devitt for
realism and a correspondence theory of truth. However, Devitt
needs to be supplemented because he is vulnerable on two
counts:

> In the first place, realism of the kind advocated by Devitt, while
> plausible from the standpoints both of common sense and
> practical science, remains entirely unaccounted for. The proper-
> ties and powers of basic matter or energy and its concretion,
> under highly specific and constant laws into the natural kinds
> which we observe around us, are accepted simply as brute facts
> by realists such as Devitt. The objectivity of the natural world is
> accepted and affirmed, but it is unexplained. In the second place,
> Devitt's metaphysical realism is vulnerable in that he also affirms
> a purely physicalist or materialist account of consciousness and
> the human mind . . . [P]hysicalism is an implausible doctrine. It
> fails to do justice to the phenomena of consciousness, let alone
> mental life and experience.[18]

Hebblethwaite's problem is this: Devitt is right to affirm that
humans can discover the truth about the world. However,
Devitt cannot really be allowed to stop here. For the capacity
to explain the world implies (a) the stability of the objective
world, and (b) the miracle of human consciousness. Both
features, argues Hebblethwaite, are best explained by reference to God. At this point, Hebblethwaite has merged his
argument from truth with the argument from design. It is
the order and stability of the world and the amazing capacity

of humans to think that reflect the intentions of a designer God. Hebblethwaite sums up:

> In a nutshell, the argument from truth to God is this: our deep-rooted conviction that truth is a matter of discovery and not invention is best accounted for – especially in its fullest scope, that is to say, including the truths of mind as well as of matter – on the supposition of an infinite creative Mind that makes things what they are and preserves them as what they are for us to discover.[19]

Hebblethwaite couples this inductive argument with a historical note about the dangers to truth when belief in God is undermined. Nietzsche is helpful to Hebblethwaite here: for Nietzsche shares the Augustinian conviction that belief (or disbelief) in God affects everything. As will be discussed later, Nietzsche seems to accept that the possibility of truth does depend on belief in God.

To sum up this section: Augustine, Anselm, and Hebblethwaite all share the conviction that the claim that God exists is not a claim about some remote object, but a conviction that affects the absolute fundamentals of being, right down to the possibility of truth. Where Hebblethwaite differs from Augustine and Anselm is in rejecting their Neoplatonic packaging. And Hebblethwaite did this by linking the argument from truth to the design argument.

I differ from Hebblethwaite in two ways. First, as discussed already, I cannot simply affirm Devitt's arguments for truth; the tradition-constituted nature of knowledge needs to be taken more seriously. Second, Hebblethwaite modernized the argument by linking it with the design argument, while I shall use the cosmological argument. The crucial move, in my judgement, is not simply to explain the order necessary for truth, but the *assumption* of order that is implied in truth. We are not simply leaping from a world which as it happens is orderly, but rather we cannot even start to talk about the world unless it is orderly. It is the assumption of coherence and intelligibility which requires justification. And this is the territory traditionally embraced by the cosmological argument.

Truth and the cosmological argument

This survey of these various arguments from truth to God has been a parenthesis in my main argument. So before developing the Thomist alternative argument from truth to God, it is necessary to recapitulate the argument as it stood at the end of the last chapter.

1. Humans live in community and successfully communicate.

This is a presupposition of MacIntyre's 'tradition-constituted enquiry'. One cannot even state the problem posed to our epistemology by language unless one assumes that this at least is the case.

2. Translation assumes that one of the major purposes of language is to explain the world. [20]

Inaccurate translations provide decisive evidence that this is so. An example already laboured is the expression 'restroom' in American which is inaccurately translated if the person is directed to the bedroom. A better example is that 'la maison' in French would be inaccurately translated by the English word 'car'. An object in reality will determine the appropriate translation.

3. Translation is evidence that (a) it is possible to describe the world, and (b) it can be difficult to describe the world.

If we concede the second point, then (a) must follow. If we concede that objects in reality determine legitimate translations, then we are committed to the possibility of better and worse descriptions. The difficulty arises because the translation experience also generates a significant number of moments when there is no corresponding word in the other language. Bilingual people live with this difficulty all the time. It arises because of the complexity of our world. The problem rarely arises with objects and animals, despite Quine's problem with rabbits, but more with feelings, dispositions, and outlooks.

The reason for this is that the latter are capturing human experiences of the world which are much more complicated and more varied and culture-related than objects.

4. *Successful communication assumes a shared set of logical categories.*

Descriptions must assume certain basic logical laws.[21] If I started identifying chairs-which-are-simultaneously-not-chairs, then all meaningful discourse would rapidly break down. Logic simply demands consistency in our use of words and in our rules of inference. It is not a strait-jacket. If a theologian (with the doctrine of the incarnation perhaps) or physicist (with quantum mechanics) starts to use words slightly differently from the normal usage, then it is acknowledged as a significant exception and demands careful explanation. In both cases, the doctrine (or theory) is not described as a contradiction but as a paradox or perhaps as a mystery transcending the powers of language and logic. Paradox is a term intended to acknowledge an apparent contradiction that is not an actual one.

5. *Logical categories must mirror the world.*

Given that we are successful in our attempts to communicate, then the most likely explanation is that the coherence reflected in our language is justified by reality. Again returning to translation, unless the coherence assumed by our language is mirrored in reality then it is always possible that nonsense translations are correct. Comparisons and judgements about better or worse translations would become impossible.

This takes us to the end of Chapter 3. The question is, how do we explain this coherence? At this point, there are two options. One simply states that it is arbitrary (i.e. it could have been chaotic, but fortunately it is not). The other believes that it is made possible by God. The problem with the first option is that it undermines a critically realist concept of truth. The reason for this can be stated in the following way:

1. Sentences are true when they form a part of the world perspective that explains the complexities of reality in a better way than the alternatives. With many assertions, this is relatively easy. I claim that there is an elephant on the lawn, and you insist it is a blackbird. Upon looking at the lawn, it is clear that a black bird is pecking at the grass. Then your description is undeniably a better one than mine. With many other assertions it is much harder. If I claim that the best explanation for crop-circles is creatures from outer space, then the arguments are much more complex. With the blackbird illustration, we are entitled to have more certainty than with the crop-circle illustration. With the latter there are legitimate grounds for disagreement and doubt. We can have what I may call existential doubt (i.e. a doubt generated by the complexity of reality). The entitlement to believe is determined by the nature of reality and the best explanation for the data.

2. If the coherence of reality is arbitrary, then it is possible that either the universe could at any moment cease being orderly or coherent, or its coherence only extends to certain parts. The major difficulty on this view is that the universe could be intrinsically chaotic and we would not realize it. If, for example, the order is all entirely mind imposed, then the actual state of the universe might be chaotic to a small or larger degree. We are left with a fundamental doubt about all claims to truth.

3. Due to the fact that we cannot exclude these two possibilities (namely, potential or partial chaos), then the maximum we are entitled to say is that 'x is true' subject to the possibility of disorder and chaos.

4. The introduction of fundamental doubt has undermined our entitlement to believe. In principle the chaos could involve different entities being the same. Even assertions about blackbirds or elephants on the lawn are now subject to doubt. We have lost the condition for critical realism: when every assertion can be doubted then reality can no longer be the arbiter among different descriptions. The

claim that the apparent coherence of the universe is arbitrary seems ultimately to push one to a denial of critical realism.

So we need an explanation for coherence that does not leave it arbitrary and fortuitous. At this point it is necessary to introduce the *tradition* of natural theology.

MacIntyre is right to describe the Enlightenment project as an attempt to discover a 'tradition-transcendent rationality'. And MacIntyre is also correct to report that the entire project was a failure. One option considered and rejected by Hume and Kant was the entire tradition of natural theology. For them, the supposed 'proofs' for the existence of God did not succeed because it was always possible to reject the premises. With regard to the design argument, explained Hume, it is always possible to insist that order in nature is not evidence of purpose, but the convenient result of chance. With regard to the cosmological argument, it is possible to hold that the world is just contingent and ultimately inexplicable. And with regard to the ontological argument, one can simply refuse the definition of God as a necessary being existing within all logically possible worlds. In other words, the requirement that the arguments work outside any tradition meant that they were doomed to failure. However, perhaps the Hume attack is completely missing the point of the arguments. Perhaps they were never intended for the person outside all traditions.

Now we return to MacIntyre, who has argued that this is the case with St Thomas. MacIntyre has suggested an alternative reading that rejects the traditional foundationalist account. Scott MacDonald summarizes the traditional reading when he writes,

> Aquinas's most detailed epistemological reflections occur in the context of his discussion of the propositional attitude *scientia*, which he conceives of as the paradigm of knowledge. To have *scientia* with respect to a given thing is to have complete and certain cognition of its truth; that is, to hold a given proposition on grounds that guarantee its truth in a certain way. Following Aristotle, Aquinas holds that grounds of this sort are provided

only by demonstrative syllogisms, and so he maintains that the objects of *scientia* are propositions one holds on the basis of demonstrative syllogisms. To have *scientia* with respect to some proposition p, then, is to have a particular sort of inferential justification for p.[22]

According to MacDonald, rational justification for St Thomas is a matter of deducing from certain self-evident first principles. It is in this way that the arguments have sufficient force to persuade all people.

Not so, retorts MacIntyre. He writes, 'What this . . . fails to take account of is the difference between rational justi- fication within science, the rational justification of a science, and the rational justification required by an account of the sciences as a whole, hierarchically ordered system.'[23] MacIntyre believes that the apparent foundationalism is a description of the method within St Thomas's tradition, not a justification of the tradition. In other words, St Thomas should be read as a person who was living, as a Dominican Friar, in the Augustinian tradition and engaging with the rediscovery of Aristotle, and then offering his reworking of the tradition from within, a reworking that St Thomas would have expected to need further development as the tradition developed. In *Three Rival Versions of Moral Enquiry*, MacIntyre speaks of the Thomist procedure as a craft – a skill to be taught in community, which is initially cultivated under authority, and is permitted to develop and blossom. MacIntyre writes,

> The standards of achievement within any craft are justified historically. They have emerged from the criticism of their predecessors and they are justified because and insofar as they have remedied the defects and transcended the limitation of those predecessors as guides to excellent achievement within that particular craft . . .Those successive partial and imperfect versions of that science or sciences, which are elaborated at different stages in the history of the craft, provide frameworks within which claimants to truth succeed or fail by finding or failing to find a place in those deductive schemes. But the overall schemes themselves are justified by their ability to do better than any rival competitors so far, both in organizing the experience

of those who have up to this point made the craft what it is and in supplying correction and improvement where some need for these has been identified.[24]

One interesting consequence of this view is that St Thomas has been misunderstood by those Roman Catholics who want to use him as the last word on all questions. The encyclical *Aeterni Patris*, issued by Pope Leo XIII in 1879, takes this line. MacIntyre blames Joseph Kleutgen for the misunderstanding. Kleutgen's mistake was to treat 'Aquinas as presenting a finished system whose indebtedness to earlier writers is no more than an accidental feature of it'.[25] Kleutgen assumed that the methodology is the same as that of Descartes and Kant; the achievement then becomes that it is simply a better set of answers. However, in fact, MacIntyre holds that the Thomist methodology is opposed to the 'tradition-transcendent' assumptions of modernity.

The tradition of natural theology should not be viewed as an exercise in seeking arguments to persuade the non-existent 'traditionless' person. Instead its role is to tease out the explanatory power of the Christian tradition. This is not done outside the tradition, but within the tradition. Yet it can be compelling for people outside the tradition, because the proofs illustrate the incomplete nature of their own tradition. However, this is to move on too quickly, so let us first examine the cosmological argument.

The cosmological argument has been formulated in several different ways, only some of which are actually found in St Thomas. I shall concentrate on the main three.[26] The first treats it as an argument about the origins of the universe. The second uses a version of Leibniz's 'Principle of Sufficient Reason'. And the third understands the argument to be an examination of the nature of intelligibility.

The first has a redoubtable defender in William Lane Craig. For Craig, the question is simple: how did the universe begin? Craig argues that the enduring Big Bang theory provides decisive empirical evidence that the universe had a beginning. The idea of the universe starting by itself from nothing is too absurd to contemplate. Therefore one needs to postulate a creator.[27] A major difficulty with this argument is in the work of Stephen Hawking. Quentin Smith makes use of Hawking to argue that his quantum cosmology provides an alternative, namely a self-contained universe, having no boundary or edge, and therefore not needing a beginning. For Hawking, the universe is finite but it did not have an origin.[28]

This entire approach could not be more misguided. It is the God of deism that simply starts the universe. The God of theism is the sustainer of all that is – then and now. God is not the great first cause, somewhere back in the mists of time. In fact, when Aquinas discusses the creation of the universe, he implies that rationally his preference is to believe, like his Greek 'masters', that matter is eternal, but on the basis of Genesis 1 he accepts that the universe had a beginning.[29] But both his cosmological argument and his faith would be intact if it were shown that the universe was infinite. Craig concedes this point in passing,[30] but fails to see that it undermines the entire enterprise of the book. John Polkinghorne places the Hawking question into the appropriate context, when he writes:

> Of course, the first thing to say about that discourse is that theology is concerned with Ontological origin and not with temporal beginning. The idea of creation has no special stake in a datable start to the universe. If Hawking is right, and quantum effects mean that the cosmos as we know it is like a kind of fuzzy spacetime egg, without a singular point at which it all began, that is scientifically very interesting, but theologically insignificant . . . Creation is not something he (i.e. God) did fifteen billion years ago, but it is something that he is doing now.[31]

Certainly the Thomist form of the cosmological argument is not particularly interested in the origin of the universe. It is closer to the second type of cosmological argument that appeals to some form of Leibniz's 'principle of sufficient reason'.[32]

Leibniz's cosmological argument works from two principles: the first is the law of contradiction; and the second is the principle of sufficient reason. The first is no problem. The second, however, is subject to much discussion. Leibniz states it as follows: 'And that of sufficient reason, in virtue of which we held that no fact can be real or existent, no statement true, unless there be a sufficient reason why it is so and not otherwise, although most often these reasons cannot be known to us.'[33] This principle has proved enormously important for understanding the structure of the cosmological argument, because almost all versions appeal to this principle in some form. So for the purposes of comparison with the argument I shall offer later, it is worth examining Leibniz's argument with care. Craig helpfully schematizes it in the following way:

1. Something exists.
2. There must be a sufficient reason or rational basis for why something exists rather than nothing.
3. This sufficient reason cannot be found in any single thing or in the whole aggregate of things or in the efficient causes of all things.
   (*a*) Things in the world are contingent, that is, determined in their being by other things such that if matter and motion were changed, they would not exist.
   (*b*) The world is simply a conglomeration of such things and is thus itself contingent.
   (*c*) The efficient causes of all things are simply prior states of the world, and these successive states do not explain why there are any states, any world, at all.
4. Therefore, there must exist outside the world and the states of the world a sufficient reason for the existence of the world.
5. This sufficient reason will be a metaphysically necessary being, that is, a being whose sufficient reason for existence is self-contained.[34]

When faced with this argument, the literature has been preoccupied with two issues. The first is the validity of the 'principle of sufficient reason'. Attacks have come from a variety of directions. Hume asked, if one has explained each part of the universe, then what further is there to explain?[35] We know that each part of the universe is explicable in terms of prior states and natural laws, and that is sufficient.

One might feel with Richard Swinburne that an explanation is required for the natural laws.[36] However, even if, with Gaskin, this is granted as a legitimate question, then Gaskin cannot see any reason why the answer cannot simply be that there is no explanation. Gaskin writes,

> What Leibniz establishes with unrivalled clarity is the insight that in the last resort explanation of the laws of change and of the existence of the physical universe (if the universe is of finite duration) cannot come from within it. What is not established is that it must come from outside. There may indeed be no explanation.[37]

The second objection rests with the conclusion. Is the idea of a metaphysically necessary being coherent? It was probably Leibniz's conclusion that provoked Kant to observe that the cosmological argument fails because, in the end, it depends on the ontological. The difficulty is that most of us find it quite easy to imagine any existing entity not existing. If anything that exists could be conceived of as not existing, then no being could be logically necessary.[38]

My third type of cosmological argument is clearly linked with the second, although it has a significantly different emphasis. The two proponents are Keith Ward and Hugo Meynell.[39] Primarily it is a reworking of Aquinas's Third Way. The Third Way is best seen as an exploration of the concept of intelligibility and explanation. This version is my own reworking of Ward and Meynell. It can be shown as follows:

1.   Whenever we experience an event, the natural human instinct is to seek an explanation. For example, most of us want to know the cause of the presence of a fallen tree blocking the road. This is a very basic human instinct.

2.   The explanations for most events are contingent. This is to say, the explanations could be otherwise and are dependent upon another layer of explanation. So, returning to our tree, after some enquiry we discover that there was a storm last night that resulted in the tree falling down. This is one explanation among several possible explanations, and it is clearly dependent on the existence of a weather-system.

3.   An infinite regress of contingent explanations would still leave the entire system unexplained (i.e. it would not be a complete explanation). The universe as *a whole* would make no sense if the explanations were contingent and infinitely regressive; any conceivable contingent explanation would lead to the next stage needing to be explained. So let us suppose, in the case of our tree, that after several layers of explanations, we arrive back at the fundamental laws of physics; the question then is: how do we explain these laws?

At this point, we note that Aquinas excludes two options. He excludes the possibility of an infinite regress of contingent explanations, because that would simply leave the universe as a whole unintelligible. He also excludes the option of simply stopping at a particular point. Bertrand Russell wanted to stop at the universe and decide that 'it is just there, that's all'.[40] But the universe is simply the sum of contingent events that still require explanation.

4.   Therefore for the universe to 'make sense', one must have a 'necessary being'. Aquinas says, 'One is forced therefore to suppose something which must be, and owes this to no other thing than itself; indeed it itself is the cause that other things must be.'[41]

It is worth pausing here to note both the similarities and differences between this form of the cosmological argument and the Leibnizian form. The similarities are, perhaps, more apparent than the differences. Using a version of the 'principle of sufficient reason', we are working from contingent events to a necessary being. It is a quest for a 'complete explanation'.

The difference is that sometimes Ward sees himself on the verge of treating the cosmological argument not as a straightforward *a posteriori* argument, but as an examination of certain assumptions. The most striking moment comes when, in his discussion of the ontological argument, he writes:

> The structure of the argument in the so-called Cosmological and Ontological proofs is thus essentially the same. Both are arguments which are primarily philosophical, not experimental: that is to say, they are concerned with analysis of certain concepts,

especially those of 'necessity', 'causality', 'explanation' and
'value'. This is not defining terms at will, but of trying to achieve
a coherent, consistent, elegant and illuminating conceptual
interpretation of reality.[42]

This is a real insight. Ward is correct to imply that the argument identifies the conditions that justify our confidence that
the world is coherent. It is like the ontological argument in
that it explores our assumptions. This is something I shall
return to.

However, most of the time this insight is obscured, and
Ward operates on assumptions suggested by Leibniz. In
dealing with the two objections already stated, Ward concedes
one but fights resolutely on the other. He concedes that
one would have to accept the assumption that it is meaningful to search for a complete explanation for the universe.
Ward writes, 'They cannot get started without the basic
assumption that there is a complete explanation for the
world.'[43] So Ward cannot persuade Russell or Gaskin to move
beyond the universe which is 'just there'. All the argument
shows is that if one asks for an explanation for the universe,
then the answer given would have to involve a 'self-
explanatory' being.

The bulk of Ward's discussion is against the second objection. What does it mean to describe God as a 'self-explanatory
being'? Certainly this being needs to be logically necessary,
so Ward has many critics to overcome. Ward takes Richard
Swinburne as a representative critic. Swinburne has argued
that the concept of what he calls 'an absolute explanation'
(i.e. an explanation which is logically necessary) is incoherent.
Swinburne writes,

> I do not believe that there can be any absolute explanations of
> logically contingent phenomena. For surely never does anything
> explain itself. P's existence at t_2 may be explained in part by P's
> existence at t_1. But P's existence at t_1 could not explain P's
> existence at t_1. P's existence at t_1 might be the ultimate brute
> fact about the universe, but it would not explain itself. Nor can
> anything logically necessary provide any explanation of anything
> logically contingent. For a full explanation is, we have seen, such
> that the *explanandum* (i.e. the phenomenon requiring explana-

tion) is deducible from it. But you cannot deduce anything logically contingent from anything logically necessary.[44]

There are two objections from Swinburne here. First, the idea of something explaining itself is incoherent. Second, the logically necessary cannot explain the contingent.

Against the first objection, Ward tries to explicate the notion. A self-explanatory being, says Ward, would be one which is 'existentially self-sufficient; that is, it can depend upon nothing other than itself for its existence.'[45] Ward correctly observes that this must be the case otherwise the being would have to be explained by reference to something else. Further this non-dependent being cannot bring itself into existence. For to do so, it would already have to exist, which is clearly contradictory. Neither can anything else bring it into existence nor can it come into existence from nothing, because that would leave the mystery about why it has a particular nature, thereby leaving something unexplained. Finally, it cannot be a complex reality with one part producing another, because one would still be left with the initial part as uncaused. So Ward concludes, 'Thus its existence can depend upon nothing, neither upon itself nor some other being. It must, therefore, always have existed; it must be uncaused, either by itself or by another.'[46]

Incoherence can be established in one of two ways. First the idea might be vacuous. Ward has shown that this is not the case. Granted that the idea is stretching human language to the limits, but this is inevitable in theology. The idea of a self-explanatory being, which if sufficient to explain all logically possible contingent worlds must be logically necessary, clearly has content. The second way is to show that the idea is self-contradictory. The above account is not obviously self-contradictory. If we can envisage the opposite (i.e. entities which are dependent and caused) then surely it is logically possible to envisage an entity non-dependent and uncaused. The onus of proof when it comes to accusations of incoherence must rest with those who make the charge. Ward has done sufficient to show that the case has not been made.

With Swinburne's second criticism that the logically necessary cannot be an explanation for a contingent universe, Ward
makes a significant concession:

> As for the necessary not entailing the contingent, that is, of
> course, quite correct . . . It clearly requires making God, the
> self-explanatory being, contingent in some respects . . . I
> think Swinburne's mistake . . . is to insist that God is either
> necessary in all respects, or contingent in all respects – just
> the ultimate contingent fact. Whereas, I shall argue, we can
> have both necessity and contingency in God. And we need
> both.[47]

The description of the concept of God affirmed by theists at
the outset of this chapter will show that I endorse such a move.
As Ward puts it, '[I]t is possible and proper to think of God
as a necessary, eternal and infinite being, who is the free
creator of everything other than himself. God is the one self-
existent being in whom creation and necessity originate and
in whom they are reconciled.'[48]

So on the cosmological argument the current position is
this: the actual steps in the argument are all defensible, *once
one decides to participate*. Ward has shown that an intelligible
universe require a logically necessary being. But he concedes
that if one decides that it is unreasonable to expect the
universe *in toto* to have an explanation, then one will not be
compelled to believe by the argument.

It is at this point that this discussion is linked with the quest
to understand the conditions that underpin language and
logic. Instead of simply starting with a certain event, we should
push the argument back. There is a prior mystery. How is it
possible that we can explain any event? How are true
descriptions of the world possible? What explanations can be
given for the coherence of reality?

The answer that the coherence is purely fortuitous and
arbitrary pushes one to anti-realism. The essential condition
for truth is undermined. The cosmological argument suggests
a different answer. The coherence of the universe implies
that events make sense (and that non-contradictory explanations for events can be given). The intelligibility of each

particular event assumes an overall coherence that requires a belief in a self-explanatory being.

The advantage of the cosmological argument becoming a part of our assumptions about the universe is that Gaskin *et al.* can no longer affirm that coherent explanations can be given for each part but not everything. This form of the cosmological argument challenges the assumption that we are otherwise in a position to explain anything at all.

In Chapter 2 MacIntyre and Milbank were set against each other. Milbank's problem was that MacIntyre must assume a shared rationality that justifies the comparative explanatory power of competing traditions. This criticism of MacIntyre I agreed with. However, this 'tradition-constituted rationality' can only be justified in the theistic traditions. These steps can be made explicit in the following ways:[49]

1. MacIntyre's 'traditioned-rationality' depends upon showing the intelligibility of the universe.
2. The intelligibility of the universe requires that the universe is ultimately explicable.
3. An endless set of contingent explanations will leave the universe as ultimately unexplained, for a contingent explanation always requires a further explanation.
4. Therefore for the universe to be intelligible, there must be a necessary being (i.e. a logically necessary being who exists in all possible worlds and is self-explanatory).
5. This is what theists mean by God.

In the first step, I am claiming that the 'critically realist instinct' is that world views attempt to make sense of human experience. 'Making sense' requires that we expect the universe to provide a coherent and stable set of experiences.

In the second step, I claim that if the universe is not ultimately explicable – if there is not an ultimate explanation – then it would be just good fortune that we are able to explain anything at all. Furthermore at any moment the contingency of the universe might destroy the regular patterns that we have so far discerned. In his argument for the Third Way, Aquinas argues that everything could suddenly cease to be.

Categories such as consistency, coherence, and evidence would appear inappropriate in a completely contingent universe.

In the third step, we have the thrust of the Thomist argument. One does not provide an ultimate explanation unless one has an explanation that is not contingent. One cannot just stop at the ultimate laws of physics because these are clearly contingent and therefore themselves require explanation. The ultimate explanation must be necessary.

With the fourth step, we introduce the concept of a necessary being. Despite certain difficulties, I have already defended the coherence of this idea. Finally, we identify this being with the God of traditional theism.

Therefore we arrive at the rather surprising conclusion that 'traditioned-rationality' depends on the 'critical realist' assumption that the world can be explained. If the intention of most world-views to explain the world is legitimate, then I have shown that a necessary being is implied. And the idea of a necessary being is part of what we mean by God. Now we are only left with two options. First, a world-view which is both realist and theist. Now this, I have shown, is coherent and reasonable. Second, a world-view which is explicitly anti-realist. Once you give up on truth and simply articulate your narrative, then you have also given up on intelligible explanations for the world, and therefore God.

One option which has disappeared is naturalism. This is the desire to explain the world without reference to God. Atheism, Marxism, and other naturalistic world-views are realist but not theistic. The argument in this chapter exposes the radical incoherence of all naturalistic philosophies. To those who continue to explain the world without believing in God, I can only suggest that they are operating with an *unjustifiable rationality* – quite literally, an irrational rationality. If they have thought through their assumptions, then the best that they can say is that they are seeking 'explanations' that, by some good fortune, *appear* to make sense. This I suspect is all that David Hume would have managed to claim. There is something manifestly problematic about offering explanations when one is uncertain that anything can be explained. It is not surprising that such *unjustifiable rationality* is always vulnerable to relativism and nihilism.

In the next chapter we shall examine the work of Nietzsche. For Nietzsche saw the dangers of relativism and nihilism with characteristic clarity.

Notes

1. There are others who have expressed sympathy with the argument from truth to God. Along with Hebblethwaite, probably the next most notable contemporary exponent is Michael Dummett. For a brief discussion see 'Truth, Time and Deity' by Brian McGuinness in Brian McGuinness and Gianluigi Oliveri (eds.), *The Philosophy of Michael Dummett* (Dordrecht: Kluwer Academic Publishers, 1994), pp. 229–39. As McGuinness observes, Dummett did not develop his provocative paper in which he argued that only on a theistic basis could one defend realism. For that reason I have not included him in this chapter.

2. Etienne Gilson, *The Christian Philosophy of Saint Augustine* translated by L. E. M. Lynch (London: Victor Gollancz, 1961).

3. See R. Douglas Geivett, *Evil and the Providence of God* (Philadelphia: Temple University Press, 1993). Geivett discusses Augustine's natural theology in chapter 2. The problem of theodicy is reduced because if, on other grounds, one is certain that God exists, then the problem of evil can no longer provide an argument for atheism.

4. The certainty of our self-knowledge emerges elsewhere in his work. In *City of God* XI, 26, one finds an argument strikingly similar to Descartes' conclusion in the *Meditations*. Augustine writes, 'Because then, even if I were mistaken, there would have to be a me to be mistaken, there can be no doubt at all, that in my knowing that I am, I am not mistaken.'

5. Augustine, *On Free Choice of the Will* translated by Thomas Williams (Indianapolis: Hackett Publishing Company, 1993), p. 41.

6. Ibid., p. 50.

7. Ibid., pp. 54–7. The quotation within is from Psalm 37:4.

8. Henry Chadwick, *Augustine* (Oxford: OUP, 1986), p. 42.

9. Augustine, *On Free Choice of the Will*, p. 31.

10. Etienne Gilson, *The Christian Philosophy of Saint Augustine*, p. 23.

11. For the background to the argument see, R. W. Southern, *Saint Anselm: A Portrait in a Landscape* (Cambridge: Cambridge University Press, 1990), pp. 113–27.

12. See M. J. Charlesworth's helpful introduction to Anselm's *Proslogion* for an extended discussion the similarities and differences between Anselm and Augustine. M. J. Charlesworth (translator and editor), *St. Anselm's Proslogion* (Oxford: Clarendon Press, 1965), pp. 23f.

13. J. Hopkins and H. Richardson (edited and translated), *Anselm of Canterbury* Volume 1 (London: SCM Press, 1974). *Monologion*, chapter 18, pp. 28–9.

14. J. Hopkins and H. Richardson (edited and translated), *Anselm of Canterbury* Volume 2 (Toronto and New York: Edwin Mellen Press, 1976), p. 102. In our post-Einstein age, the time illustration is wholly inappropriate. We now know that, in fact, everything has its own time, because time is relational and linked to motion and space.

15. G. R. Evans, *Anselm* (London: Geoffrey Chapman, 1989), p. 37.

16. B. L. Hebblethwaite, *The Ocean of Truth* (Cambridge: Cambridge University Press, 1988), p. 111.

17. Ibid., p. 111.

18. Ibid., p. 108.

19. Ibid., p. 110.

20. Language does have other purposes, for example, admonition and prescription.

21. This is not to imply that we need to share all logical categories. However, where there is a disagreement about these categories, then one is likely to find some confusion and misunderstanding.

22. Scott Macdonald, 'Aquinas, Thomas' in J. Dancy and E. Sosa (eds.), *A Companion to Epistemology* (Oxford: Basil Blackwell, 1992), p. 19.

23. Alasdair MacIntyre, *Whose Justice? Which Rationality?* p. 173.

24. Alasdair MacIntyre, *Three Rival Versions of Moral Enquiry Encylopaedia, Genealogy, and Tradition* (London: Duckworth, 1990), p. 64.

25. Ibid., p. 74.

26. William L. Craig in *The Cosmological Argument from Plato to Leibniz* (Basingstoke: Macmillan, 1980) suggests a different taxonomy. He writes as follows, 'During the historical survey of the argument, my attention was drawn to one very important feature of the cosmological proof: the role of the infinite regress in the argument. If we use this feature as our criterion we can

categorise the arguments into three types: (1) those that maintain the impossibility of an infinite temporal regress, (2) those that maintain the impossibility of an infinite essentially ordered regress, and (3) those that have no reference to an infinite regress at all' (p. 282). The problem with this taxonomy is that the second and the third are largely the same. Into the second, Craig places Aquinas's five ways and into the third he places Leibniz's 'principle of sufficient reason'. I am not persuaded by his arguments that these two ought to be separated. And most Thomists merge the two.

27. See W. L. Craig and Q. Smith, *Theism, Atheism, and Big Bang Cosmology* (Oxford: Clarendon Press, 1993), chapter 1.

28. Ibid., chapter 11.

29. See St Thomas, *Summa Theologiae*, 1a, Question 46, article 3, translated by T. McDermott (London: Blackfriars, 1964), p. 79.

30. W. L. Craig and Q. Smith, *Theism, Atheism, and Big Bang Cosmology*, p. 283.

31. J. Polkinghorne, *Science and Christian Belief* (London: SPCK, 1994), p. 73.

32. William Craig has challenged this reading of Aquinas. For reasons that will become apparent, I think he is wrong to insist that the reading offered by most Thomists is inappropriate. For W. L. Craig see *The Cosmological Argument from Plato to Leibniz*, p. 285.

33. Leibniz as cited in W. L. Craig, *The Cosmological Argument from Plato to Leibniz*, p. 258.

34. Ibid., p. 274.

35. See David Hume, *Dialogues Concerning Natural Religion* (London: Hafner Press, 1948), pp. 59f.

36. See R. Swinburne, *The Existence of God* (Oxford: Clarendon Press, 1979), pp. 126f. Swinburne seems to opt for a very weak form of the cosmological argument. Owing to his difficulties with a necessary being, he cannot opt for Leibniz's position. So, instead, he suggests that it is just more likely that there is a God who decides to create a complex universe than that the universe is uncaused. The problem with this is it does depend on accepting his quantification. This is the point that John Hick makes very effectively in his *An Interpretation of Religion* (Basingstoke: Macmillan, 1989), p. 104–9.

37. J. C. A. Gaskin, *The Quest for Eternity* (Harmondsworth: Penguin, 1984), pp. 64–5.

38. David Hume made this point in Part 9 of his *Natural Dialogues Concerning Religion*. An interesting variant on this criticism is found in Richard Gale's highly entertaining book *On the Nature and Existence of God* (Cambridge: Cambridge University Press, 1991). He thinks that the idea of an 'unsurpassably great being' is extremely complex and problematic. He doubts whether a coherent account of God can be given.

39. I shall be concentrating on Ward's presentation rather than Meynell's. However, it is worth noting that Meynell's highly original treatment of the cosmological argument anticipates in many ways the work of Brian Hebblethwaite. For Meynell, see *The Intelligible Universe* (London: Macmillan, 1982).

40. B. Russell, *Why I am not a Christian* (London: Unwin Books, 1967), p. 140.

41. St Thomas Aquinas, *Summa Theologiae*, 1a, Question 2, article 3.

42. K. Ward, *Rational Theology and the Creativity of God* (Oxford: Basil Blackwell, 1982), p. 31.

43. Ibid., p. 5.

44. R. Swinburne, *The Existence of God*, p. 76.

45. K. Ward, *Rational Theology and the Creativity of God*, p. 10.

46. Ibid., p. 10.

47. Ibid., p. 8.

48. Ibid., p. 3.

49. Meynell's summary of the cosmological argument is very similar to the argument I am offering here. The slight differences are, first, I follow MacIntyre in accepting that knowledge is tradition-constituted; and, second, Meynell's concept of God I find unnecessarily anthropomorphic. For Meynell see *The Intelligible Universe*, p. 118.

CHAPTER 5

Nietzsche and truth

Many have noted the great irony of modernity: we are the age of dramatic scientific discoveries while at the same time deciding that we know nothing. With Newton and Darwin, we have the explosion of scientific knowledge, while with Hume and Lessing, we have decided that we have no sure way of knowing anything.

Modernity's solution to this irony was offered by Kant. The crucial distinction embedded in *The Critique of Pure Reason* between the phenomenal and the noumenal enabled the two elements of modernity to coexist in awkward tension.[1] Science, explained Kant, completely explained the phenomenal (the world as it appeared to the mind); however, this is not knowledge of the noumenal (the way things are in them-selves). This meant that we thought we had knowledge – which, ultimately, was not knowledge. This was always a fragile solution. And Nietzsche is the person who exposed its in-adequacy.

Before we proceed any further, perhaps it would be helpful to locate oneself on the increasingly confusing map of Nietzschian studies. The range of interpretations of Nietzsche's work is considerable.[2] Nietzsche's work has been viewed with considerable suspicion because of the use made of it by Hitler and the Nazis. He was apparently Hitler's favourite philosopher. It was thanks to Walter Kaufmann that this suspicion was overcome and Nietzsche was liberated from such associations. Kaufmann turned Nietzsche into a relatively straightforward humanist existentialist and pragmatist, who denies all metaphysics, including its Platonic, Christian, and Kantian forms, and then confronts the ethical implications of such a denial.[3] The problem with this interpretation is that there are just too many parts of Nietzsche which are much more radical. Repeatedly he denies the possibility of all knowledge, describing science as 'an interpretation and arrangement of the world . . . and not an explanation of the world'.[4] This had led to the quest for the 'new Nietzsche', with which I am in sympathy. On this view Nietzsche's views on truth are much more radical. Richard Rorty interprets him as a radical challenge to all forms of 'realism';[5] and Jacques Derrida feels that Nietzsche exemplifies the inevitable contradiction that anyone who is trying to subvert the transcendent assumptions of language from within will get into.[6] Although I would not entirely agree with either Rorty or Derrida, I do accept that the heart of the Nietzschian message is a radical challenge to truth as traditionally understood. In addition, I hope to show that Nietzsche comes very close to affirming the theme of this book. He shares my conviction that a critically realist understanding of truth is dependent on God. Once God goes, this understanding of truth goes.

Nietzsche has left a considerable corpus of writing, and he covers a range of themes: the need to regenerate European culture; the nature of education; the implications of science for our view of ourselves; a 'yes to life'; the nature of morality; the death of God – and many more.[7] He uses wit, irony, and hyperbole to make his point. Stylistically, he is confusing. He does not provide a neat, clear, exposition of an argument for a position.[8] Indeed his style is part of the problem of interpreting Nietzsche. Because of this, along with the Hitler association already mentioned, analytic philosophers had a further reason to be suspicious. On the grounds of style alone, many conventional philosophers have simply ignored him: if he cannot state his arguments with clarity, then he does not deserve to be read. Others decide to play down his style, take a strand of Nietzsche's work, and restate it in a way that is, at least, coherent.[9]

The problem with this is that Nietzsche's style is clearly part of his message. In *Ecce Homo*, he comments explicitly on his style:

> I shall at the same time also say a general word on my art of style. To communicate a state, an inner tension of pathos through signs, including the tempo of these signs – that is the meaning of every style; and considering that the multiplicity of inner states is in my case extraordinary, there exists in my case the possibility of many styles – altogether the most manifold art of style any man has ever had at his disposal. Every style is good which actually communicates an inner state, which makes no mistake as to the signs, the tempo of the signs, the gestures – all rules of phrasing are art of gesture. My instinct is here infallible. – Good style in itself – a piece of pure folly, mere 'idealism', on a par with the 'beautiful in itself', the 'good in itself', the 'thing in itself'. . .[10]

Nietzsche here contrasts his style with 'good style' (i.e. good arguments). The problem with good argument is that it is pure folly: it is comparable with other equally foolish ideas like reality or goodness. The style is internalized. He talks elsewhere in *Ecce Homo* of the pain involved in writing and his capacity to intuit, even 'to smell'.[11] Now I want to suggest that Nietzsche's style is forced on him. In this, at least, Derrida is right. Derrida writes, 'Nietzsche might well be a little lost in the web of the text, lost much as a spider who finds he is unequal to the web he has spun.'[12] And Derrida concedes that because of Nietzsche's radical view of 'truth', Nietzsche has to rest content with the corollary that if there is no 'truth' then there is no 'truth' in Nietzsche's philosophy. Derrida uses the image of woman to represent Nietzsche's view of truth: 'There is no such thing as a woman, as a truth in itself of woman in itself. That much, at least, Nietzsche has said . . . For just this reason then, there is no such thing either as the truth of Nietzsche, or of Nietzsche's text.'[13] This is the heart of the Nietzschien problem. He feels that deductive arguments are now powerless. The assumptions necessary for such arguments are no longer available. If this is the case, then he had no option but to offer bursts of personal insight in the form of stories, aphorisms and statements. Logic assumes the intelligibility of the world: we no longer know this. Therefore we can no longer argue in these ways. Unfortunately, Nietzsche cannot simply argue (as I have just done in the preceding sentences) that argument is now impossible. An argument that argument is impossible is obviously self-refuting. Nietzsche wants to avoid this. He avoids this by refusing to say anything quite so clear. We are exhorted simply to recognize, to see, and to feel. To appreciate his position, we now need to attend to his texts with some care.

When the madman lights a lantern and runs to the market place, Nietzsche makes it quite clear that the catastrophic impact of the 'death of God' leaves nothing untouched.

> The madman jumped into their midst and pierced them with his eyes. 'Whither is God?' he cried: 'I will tell you. We have killed him – you and I. All of us are his murderers. But how did we do this? How could we drink up the sea? Who gave us the sponge to wipe away the entire horizon?'[14]

On the whole, most commentators have interpreted this famous passage as simply meaning that the 'death of God' has led to the death of conventional morality. Indeed this is the focus of most of Nietzsche's writing. However, the images here are much more dramatic. The image of the entire horizon disappearing is a striking one. Every fixed point has gone. We have murdered God but we are not facing up to the implications. Those that do face up to the implications, appear mad. The image of madness, I want to suggest, is provoked by the inability to argue.

This interpretation of Nietzsche depends on disentangling at least three meanings of the word 'truth' in Nietzsche's writings. The first meaning is *the way things are for us as historical persons in a post scientific age*. When Nietzsche writes about a changed situation, which is a result of our historical and scientific sensitivities, he believes this is something we must simply accept. Something we cannot avoid nor evade nor deny. The second meaning is *the way things really are*. This is a claim to absolute knowledge or to understand reality or metaphysics. Nietzsche attacks, unrelentingly, this conception. This is a metaphysical truth – a realist truth – and anyone who accepts the correspondence theory of truth is deluded. The third meaning is *the way we ought to be*. Here truth becomes ethical: it is a way of coping with the modern predicament.

Although Nietzsche's argument is, by definition, difficult to formulate clearly, we can summarize it thus: we live in a scientific age, which means that we live in a universe without God, where everything evolved (meaning 1). If everything evolved, then human minds and logic must have evolved too. Given this genesis for rationality itself, it is impossible that anything can be 'true' in an absolute sense. We are historical people with partial perspectives that impose order on our experience (meaning 2). This awareness will free us from the shackles of metaphysics; it should be liberating; so we need to redefine truth in order to affirm life (meaning 3).

Against Maudemarie Clark, I am not persuaded that there is a dramatic shift in Nietzsche's understanding of truth between *Beyond Good and Evil* and *The Genealogies of Morality*.[15] Instead I hold the view that Nietzsche continuously moves between these three meanings of 'truth', often in the same book. This is not to say that one cannot trace development in Nietzsche's writing. It is undoubtedly the case that he is much more persuaded of the significance of science in his early work and more wide-ranging in his later work. Yet he always retains diverse elements in constant tension, both in his earlier and in his more mature work. When exploring his writings, I shall attempt to identify the view of truth he is either presupposing or attacking. It is perhaps important to note that in some of the cases I shall now examine, he does not always use the word 'truth', but he makes it clear that he is taking a certain position which seems to correspond to one of the three options outlined above.

With the exception of his essay 'On Truth and Lies in a Nonmoral Sense' (1873), I do not propose to use the *Nachlass*, the extensive resource of notes, fragments, and essays, which Nietzsche himself did not publish. As a resource for the theme of truth, there is much within it that would assist my argument. However, Nietzschean scholars are divided over its value. Nietzsche himself clearly thought that his books were sufficient, repeatedly stressing their importance. As there is sufficient in his major works to establish my argument, I have put the *Nachlass* to one side.[16]

This chapter is not intended as an exhaustive survey of every reference to truth in Nietzsche's work.[17] For my purposes, I shall confine the discussion to the following texts: 'On Truth and Lies in a Nonmoral Sense' (1873), *Human, All Too Human* (1878), *The Gay Science* (1882), *Thus Spake Zarathustra* (1883), *Beyond Good and Evil* (1886), and *Twilight of the Idols* (1888). The aim is to show how Nietzsche moves between the three meanings of truth, thus illustrating his conviction that with the 'death of God' we have lost a realist understanding of truth.

'On Truth and Lies in a Nonmoral Sense' captures the oscillation between the first two meanings of truth. Nietzsche is preoccupied with the origins of rationality. He starts the article by musing on the way that the human capacity to know has created a certain vanity. It is difficult to illustrate, explains Nietzsche, 'how miserable, how shadowy and transient, how aimless and arbitrary the human intellect looks within nature. There were eternities during which it did not exist.'[18] At this stage, Nietzsche is assuming that evolutionary science is true (meaning 1). As one reads on, we are offered some of the standard arguments for scepticism: all humans do is

> glide over the surface of things and see 'forms'. Their senses nowhere lead to *truth*; on the contrary, they are content to receive stimuli and, as it were, to engage in a groping game on the back of things. Moreover, man permits himself to be deceived in his dreams every night of his life.[19]

Nietzsche's use of the word truth here is clearly meant in the second sense. Truth has become unknowable. The rest of the essay is preoccupied with this unknowable truth. He is puzzled as to where the quest for truth can come from. So 'the "thing in itself" (which is precisely what the pure truth, apart from any consequences, would be) is likewise something quite incomprehensible to the creator of language and something not in the least worth striving for.'[20] Language, for Nietzsche, creates the illusion of knowledge, because it imposes order on experience. But to suggest it is really knowledge is, for

Nietzsche, absurd. At the heart of the essay, he provides a definition of, what I am calling, his second meaning:

> What then is truth? A movable host of metaphors, metonymies, and anthropomorphisms: in short, a sum of human relations which have been poetically and rhetorically intensified, trans-ferred, and embellished, and which, after long usage, seems to a people fixed, canonical, and binding. Truths are illusions which we have forgotten are illusions; they are metaphors that have become worn out and have been drained of sensuous force, coins which have lost their embossing and are now considered as metal and no longer as coins.'[21]

Thus far then, Nietzsche seems to be arguing that what we now know is that truth is not knowable. 'True' statements once had power; now they are considered metal and no longer as coins. To the obvious question: How can it be true that there is no truth? he provides no answer. He cannot.

The rest of the essay examines the social nature of language and its implications for truth. These are further arguments for his second meaning. Given that society invents the categories (to take his example, we provide a definition of 'mammal'), it is no achievement to find an example and pronounce that we have discovered the 'truth'. This is a 'thoroughly anthropomorphic truth which contains not a single point which would be "true in itself" or really and universally valid apart from man'.[22]

Nietzsche in this essay has moved from the truth (meaning 1) of naturalism (i.e. there is no God – an evolutionary view of life is entirely true) to the implications for truth (meaning 2). To complain that this is manifestly self-refuting is to miss the point. For Nietzsche, this is us. He is describing our predicament. It is this predicament that we find in all his work.

Human, All Too Human was Nietzsche's second book. It broke all the conventions of traditional academic study, thereby anticipating Nietzsche's famous style. He starts this volume by distinguishing between two types of philosophy: metaphysical philosophy which produces truths (meaning 2) which are no longer believable; and historical philosophy which produces truths whose implications encapsulate our modern dilemma (meaning 1). The question is the same as in 'On Truth and Lies in a Nonmoral Sense': 'how can something originate in its opposite, for example rationality in irrationality, the sentient in the dead, logic in unlogic, disinterested contemplation in covetous desire, living for others in egoism, truth in error?'[23] Metaphysical philosophy solves the problem by referring to the transcendent: historical philosophy knows that the answer is found in chemistry. So Nietzsche writes, 'All we require, and what can be given us only now the individual sciences have attained their present level, is a *chemistry* of the moral, religious and aesthetic conceptions and sensations . . .'[24]

Nietzsche is here assuming the truth (meaning 1) of our post-Darwinian age. It is the implications of that which now occupy him. He moves on to argue that there is nothing that could be said to be true of every human, and slips into the second meaning of truth: 'But everything has become: there are no eternal facts, just as there are no absolute truths.'[25]

This distinction between Nietzsche's three meanings of the word 'truth', can help to illuminate some of the puzzles of Nietzschean scholarship. As a general rule, Nietzsche treats science as 'true' in the first sense – the way things are for us as historical persons now – and religion as not 'true' in the second sense – the way things really are. However, we do find exceptions. One such example is in section 9 of *Human, All too Human*. Nietzsche writes:

> Metaphysical world. – It is true, there could be a metaphysical
> world; the absolute possibility of it is hardly to be disputed . . .
> that possibility still remains over; but one can do absolutely
> nothing with it, not to speak of letting happiness, salvation, and
> life depend on the gossamer of such a possibility.'[26]

This overt affirmation of agnosticism has puzzled many commentators. Elsewhere Nietzsche is a consistent atheist; 'God is dead' means God is no longer available as a cultural option. Yet here he admits the possibility of metaphysics. I want to suggest that Nietzsche is now implying truth with meaning number 1, with a view to advocating truth in meaning number 2. From the perspective of modernity, it is possible there *could* be a metaphysical world (i.e. the way things are does not entirely exclude the possibility of metaphysics – meaning 1); but due to the rise of science it would be a useless world about which we cannot know anything (i.e. ultimately we would know nothing – meaning 2). Granted, this is unusual: normally science alone enjoys meaning 1, and metaphysics is confined to meaning 2. However (to anticipate a later discussion), he does the same thing in respect to science in *Beyond Good and Evil*, where he writes:

> It is perhaps just dawning on five or six minds that physics too is only an interpretation and arrangement of the world (according to our own requirements, if I may say so!) and not an explanation of the world: but in so far as it is founded on belief in the senses it passes for more than that and must continue to do so for a long time to come.[27]

Again commentators find this confusing. But once these three different meanings of truth are disentangled, then Nietzsche is here treating science using the second meaning of truth. So despite the fact that science conditions us – its influence is impossible to escape – it is not in an absolute sense 'true' (meaning 2). So, in every case, when determining Nietzsche's meaning we have to try and establish his intent. Nietzsche concedes metaphysical agnosticism when looking at our cultural position, and treats science as a construct when one is asking about its absolute truth.

Returning to *Human, All too Human*, there is one other theme that is important for our purposes. Nietzsche returns to the question of the evolutionary origins of rationality. We recognize one of the themes of 'Truth and Lies in a Nonmoral Sense' here. Language creates the illusion of control and knowledge. It also creates the foundation for logic. So Nietzsche writes:

> The sculptor of language was not so modest as to believe that he was only giving things designations, he conceived rather that with words he was expressing supreme knowledge of things; language is, in fact, the first stage of the occupation with science. Here, too, it is the belief that the truth has been found out of

which the mightiest sources of energy have flowed. A great deal later – only now – it dawns on men that in their belief in language they have propagated a tremendous error. Happily, it is too late for the evolution of reason, which depends on this belief, to be again put back. – Logic too depends on presuppositions with which nothing in the real world corresponds, for example on the presupposition that there are identical things, that the same thing is identical at different points of time.[28]

Nietzsche plainly enjoys the irony that the rationality that made science possible has been destroyed by science. It is not simply that we are no longer sure that the presuppositions of logic are justified, but that science has made them impossible to justify. He clarifies why this is the case, when he writes:

The first stage of the logical is the judgement: and the essence of the judgement consists, according to the best logicians, in belief. At the bottom of all belief there lies the sensation of the pleasurable or painful in respect to the subject experiencing the sensation.[29]

Although logic aspires to be universal, Nietzsche explains, it cannot be. All beliefs are from a perspective: the perspective in our case is the human one. So 'in our primary condition, all that interests us organic beings in any thing is its relationship to us in respect of pleasure and pain. . . . To the plants all things are usually in repose, eternal, everything identical with itself.'[30] A plant logic, Nietzsche seems to imply, would be entirely different. However, unlike plants, we believe we enjoy decision, choice, and freedom. However:

[B]elief in the freedom of the will is a primary error committed by everything organic, as old as the impulse to the logical itself; belief in unconditioned substances and in identical things is likewise a primary, ancient error committed by everything organic. Insofar, however, as all metaphysics has had principally to do with substance and freedom of will, one may designate it as the science that treats of the fundamental errors of mankind – but does so as though they were fundamental truths.[31]

Towards the end of this chapter, he returns to the issue of the illogical character of humanity. The illogical is the natural state, which we from time to time inevitably recover. He writes, 'we are from the very beginning illogical and thus unjust beings and can recognise this: this is one of the greatest and most irresolvable discords of existence.'[32]

Human, All Too Human is constantly working between the first two meanings of truth. It is true that science has transformed our self-understanding. This means that logic and rationality are unsustainable. He has no problem in celebrating reason because it gave birth to science, which in turn has liberated us from the life-destroying features of metaphysics. Nietzsche is able to claim: 'The greatest advance mankind has made lies in its having learned to draw correct conclusions.'[33] So reason is celebrated because it made possible the rise of science which in turn destroyed religion. Even though logic also has been destroyed, Nietzsche is always willing to give credit where credit is due.[34]

His next substantial discussion of reason and rationality is found in *The Gay Science*, Book 2. We recognize the problem: science generates an anthropology which does not justify the realist view of truth. We are passionate, emotional animals: yet knowledge requires dispassionate detachment. A realist is a sober person who cannot admit to being drunk. So he writes: 'To the realists – You sober people who feel well armed against passion and fantasies and would like to turn your emptiness into a matter of pride and an ornament: you call yourself realists and hint that the world really is the way it appears to you.'[35] For these realists, the problem is that 'realism' is not justified by our knowledge of what we are (meaning 1); we are passionate, drunk people. Both the realist and the non-realist have their origins in nature.'There is no "reality" for us – not for you either, my sober friends. We are not nearly as different as you think, and perhaps our good will to transcend intoxication is as respectable as your faith that you are altogether incapable of intoxication.'[36] Nietzsche is here introducing a third state, which corresponds with my third 'truth'. We have the realists (who imagine that they will never get drunk), the passionate animals (who are drunk – i.e. recognize their ontology), and Nietzsche and allies (who are trying to transcend intoxication). The passionate animals have truth number 1; the realists are guilty of believing truth

number 2; while Nietzsche is going to advocate a new way
(truth number 3).

This new response he sketches out in section 58:

> Only as creators! – This has given me the greatest trouble and
> still does: to realise that what things are called is incomparably
> more important than what they are . . . What at first was
> appearance becomes in the end, almost invariably, the essence
> and is effective as such. How foolish it would be to suppose that
> one only need to point out this origin and this misty shroud of
> delusion in order to destroy the world that counts for real, so-
> called 'reality'. We can destroy only as creators. – But let us not
> forget this either: it is enough to create new names and
> estimations and probabilities in order to create in the long run
> new 'things'.[37]

So now language provides the way forward. Naming creates
the problem; however, naming also provides the solution. For
Nietzsche, it is the recognition of this power within each of
us that provides the antidote to nihilism. No longer does a
reality (God or even science) control us, but we can become
the controllers. All we can do is interpret the signs that make
up experience: once we imagined the interpretation was given,
now Nietzsche believes we must give it. The Nietzschean circle
is now complete: science provides a historical given (a self-
understanding we must live with) – meaning 1; the historical
sensitivity has made the traditional understanding of truth
unintelligible – meaning 2; we must now seize the moment,
say yes to life, and impose our will on the world around us –
meaning 3.

Nietzsche's most frequent argument against 'realist' truth
is the anthropology generated by science. However, he provides a second argument, which is stronger. This is the
argument from the assumptions necessary for knowledge. We
find this stated in Book 3 of *The Gay Science*.

Nietzsche believes that knowledge is an inherited acqui-
sition of a species. The older an idea the greater the strength
of that idea. Most of the things humans claim to know
and have long known are errors (e.g. belief in God). However, some claims seem more useful and logic is one such.
But the problem with logic, Nietzsche explains, is that it

depends on a timeless concept of both humanity and the world. So:

> But in order to claim all this, they had to deceive themselves about their own state: they had to attribute to themselves, fictitiously, impersonality and changeless duration; they had to misapprehend the nature of the knower; they had to deny the role of the impulses of knowledge; and quite generally they had to conceive of reason as a completely free and spontaneous activity. They shut their eyes to the fact that they, too, had arrived at their propositions through opposition to common sense, or owing to a desire for tranquillity, for sole possession, or for dominion.[38]

This is not quite the same as the argument I have outlined in Chapter 3. But there are certain similarities: my argument is that logic 'fits' the world, which must imply that the world is intelligible, and that therefore there must be a God. Nietzsche starts at the other end. He knows the world is in a constant state of flux; all humans are subject to impulses of passion. He writes, 'The course of logical ideas and inferences in our brain today corresponds to a process and a struggle among impulses that are, taken singly, very illogical and unjust.'[39] The problem, for Nietzsche, is that logic assumes a timelessness both in the world and on the part of the knower. We both share a sense that logic needs to 'fit' the world. We differ in that I have argued that this requirement needs a framework of assumptions, while Nietzsche seems to think it needs some sort of immutability which is, in his view, simply not available.

He revisits all these arguments against logic in *Beyond Good and Evil*. Here his response is clearer: psychology will illuminate the process of knowing. The logician assumes a control by the knower over the known. But this is false. Nietzsche writes:

> As for the superstitions of the logicians, I shall never tire of underlining a concise little fact which these superstitious people are loath to admit – namely, that a thought comes when 'it' wants, not when 'I' want; so that it is a falsification of the facts to say: the subject 'I' is the condition of the predicate 'think'.[40]

The answer is for logicians to relinquish their expertise over 'knowing' to the psychologists. 'All psychology has hitherto remained anchored to moral prejudices and timidities: it has not ventured into the depths . . . For psychology is now once again the road to the fundamental problems.'[41] Once again, we see a true science (meaning 1) undermining the logic assumed by truth (meaning 2). The first causes the second.

In book five of *The Gay Science*, Nietzsche tackles the issue of the origins of knowledge. Here he suggests that claims to knowledge are ways of containing the world: we domesticate the unknown and strange by calling it 'known'. Nietzsche writes,

> Look, isn't our need for knowledge precisely this need for the familiar, the will to uncover under everything strange, unusual, and questionable something that no longer disturbs us? Is it not the instinct of fear that bids us to know? And is the jubilation of those who attain knowledge not the jubilation over the restoration of a sense of security?[42]

He is here commending an ethic that takes the risk of living with the lack of certainty that a life without truth (meaning 2) will entail. He is setting the scene for *Thus Spake Zarathustra*.

Primarily, *Thus Spake Zarathustra* is the development of our third meaning of truth. R. J. Hollingdale is right in his summary of the book, when he writes:

> To give life a meaning: that has been the grand endeavour of all who have preached 'truth'; for unless life is given a meaning it has none. At this level, truth is not something that can be proved or disproved: it is something which you *determine upon*, which, in the language of the old psychology, you *will*. It is not something waiting to be discovered, something to which you submit or at which you halt: it is something you *create*, it is the expression of a particular kind of life and being which has, in you, ventured to assert itself . . . What then ultimately is the answer to Pilate's question? It is: truth is will to power.[43]

In my view Nietzsche builds on meanings 1 and 2. The Superman is the person who accepts our historical position (meaning 1), is ready to grasp the implications (meaning 2), and then is able to create the meaning for the way forward. The book starts with the pronouncement by Zarathustra that God is dead. Then we have the first sermon preached to people assembled in the market square. The madness of the message is still there. Zarathustra concludes his message by saying, 'Behold, I teach you the Superman: he is this lightning, he is this madness!'[44] Madness captures the radical message (a truth where truth is not possible). But the madness is cleansing: 'Where is the madness, with which you should be cleansed?'[45] And it is controlled, because truth is to be redefined: 'Behold, I teach you the Superman. The Superman is the meaning of the earth. Let your will say: The Superman shall be the meaning of the earth!'[46] Meaning is no longer discovered, but imposed. The Superman has found the answer. It is the next development in human evolutionary history: it is, in short, the only response to our historical situation.

The three meanings of truth pervade *Thus Spake Zarathustra*. The backdrop remains the current scientific situation – a world in which God is dead. Truth, in any absolute sense, remains impossible. Nietzsche actually says that the whole message might be a deception. At the end of Part 1, Zarathustra's disciples are instructed to go away: 'Truly, I advise you: go away from me and guard yourself against Zarathustra! And better still: be ashamed of him! Perhaps he has deceived you.'[47] So Nietzsche reintroduces, at the heart of his argument in this book, his absolute scepticism about truth. Yet throughout this book, he is commending a new vision of truth: one that enables humans to take control.

In my judgement, the doctrine of the eternal recurrence should be interpreted as a part of this redefined truth of control.[48] For Nietzsche, truth becomes that which can help to affirm life. Truth is no longer the description of the way things are. Nietzsche himself, in *Ecce Homo*, interpreted the doctrine as the ultimate affirmation of every moment of life.[49] In brief, live every moment as if you will live it a million times. On this view, it is not intended to be a metaphysical claim. This has the advantage of being consistent with his work both before and after *Thus Spake Zarathustra*.

Beyond Good and Evil was his next major study. We have already noted his arguments against logic and his explicit suggestion that science is 'an arrangement'. One further insight that Nietzsche provides in this work is his vision of the new philosophy and of philosophers. Once again he makes it clear that he is building on the denial of truth in the second sense. He plays with the possibility that even the world of 'appearance' is an illusion. Hence there is no criterion by which to judge true and false. He writes:

> Indeed what compels us to assume there exists any essential antithesis between 'true' and 'false'? Is it not enough to suppose grades of apparentness and as it were lighter and darker shades and tones of appearance – different *valeurs*, to speak in the language of painters? Why could the world *which is of any concern to us* – not be a fiction?[50]

Nietzsche is now at his most radical. Essential conditions for language and knowledge are now disintegrating. It will, indeed, take a new philosopher to cope with this new situation. The new philosophers might be 'attempters'. These philosophers will be very free spirits. And what sort of truth will they preach? Here he operates with meaning number 3:

> Are they new friends of 'truth', these coming philosophers? In all probability: for all philosophers have hitherto loved their truths. But certainly they will not be dogmatists. It must offend their pride, and also their taste, if their truth is supposed to be a truth for everyman, which has hitherto been the secret desire and hidden sense of all dogmatic endeavours. 'My judgement is *my* judgement: another cannot easily acquire a right to it' – such a philosopher of the future may perhaps say.[51]

To hold to 'truth' in the sense of number 2 is to be a dogmatist. This offends 'their pride' and 'taste'. Nietzsche is resting content with the new philosophers being artists who paint their pictures, which others might like.

This radicalism in respect to a denial of realist truth anticipates one of the most famous passages in Nietzsche, which is found in the *Twilight of Idols*, 'How the "True World" Finally Became a Fiction'. This is worth quoting in full:

1.   The true world, attainable for the wise, the devout, the virtuous – they live in it, *they are it.*

(Oldest form of the idea, relatively, clever, simple, convincing. Paraphrase of the assertion, 'I, Plato, *am* the truth.')

2. The true world, unattainable for now, but promised to the wise, the devout, the virtuous ('to the sinner who does penance').

    (Progress of the idea: it becomes more refined, more devious, more mystifying – *it becomes woman*, it becomes Christian . . .)

3. The true world, unattainable, unprovable, unpromisable, but a consolation, an obligation, an imperative, merely by virtue of being thought.

    (The old sun basically, but glimpsed through fog and skepticism; the idea become sublime, pallid, Nordic, Königsbergian.)

4. The true world – unattainable? In any case, unattained. And if it is unattained, it is also *unknown*. And hence it is not consoling, redeeming, or obligating either; to what could something unknown obligate us? . . . (Gray dawn. First yawnings of reason. Rooster's crow of positivism.)

5. The 'true world' – an idea with no use anymore, no longer even obligating – an idea become useless, superfluous, *hence* a refuted idea: let's do away with it!

    (Bright day; breakfast; return of *bon sens* [good sense] and cheerfulness; Plato blushes; pandemonium of all free spirits.)

6. We have done away with the true world: what world is left over? The apparent one, maybe? . . . But no! *Along with the true world, we have also done away with the apparent!*

    (Midday; moment of the shortest shadow; end of the longest error; high point of humanity; INCIPIT ZARATHUSTRA.)[52]

This is the history of the second concept of truth. Initially absolute truth was located in the Forms (Plato); then it became idealized in Christian theology. With Kant, its demise started. Kant required metaphysics as the justification for life-denying morality. Positivism was the next stage; and finally Nietzsche arrived with the complete liberation from the bondage of realist truth.

The argument of this chapter is that Nietzsche joins Augustine and Aquinas in believing that God is required for truth. The denial of God has created the crisis of modernity. It will be objected that Nietzsche has ended up in an absurd position: you cannot argue for a position that makes argument impossible. But this is indeed Nietzsche's dilemma. He is like a person stuck in a maze, which is so complicated that all language of direction becomes completely meaningless for him.

For Nietzsche, the 'death of God' creates the context. Modernity is our situation. Science has turned us into 'apes'. Facing up to this has created the impossibility of discourse. Argument, logic, truth itself have all become absurd. It is for this reason that Derrida captures the spirit of Nietzsche's philosophy well. Derrida has inherited the style of Nietzsche. Derrida's essay 'Spurs, Nietzsche's Styles', is a masterful engagement with the Nietzschean view of truth. Derrida makes Nietzsche's allusions to 'truth as a woman' central to his argument. Derrida writes:

> For him, truth is like a woman. It resembles the veiled movement of feminine modesty. Their complicity, the complicity (rather than unity) between woman, life, seduction, modesty – all the veiled and veiling effects (Schleier, Enthüllung, Verhüllung) – is developed in a rarely quoted fragment of Nietzsche's.[53]

Derrida makes imaginative use of the 'woman' image. She knows that there is nothing ultimately to know; but men keep trying to imagine that they know her.

Later in the essay, we can find in Derrida my three different meanings of 'truth'. Derrida writes, 'Since she is a model for truth she is able to display the gifts of her seductive power, which rules over dogmatism, and dissonants and routs those credulous men, the philosophers.'[54] So in the first place woman is a model of truth, who is able to display her seductive power. This is our historical situation: a truth that 'rules over dogmatism.' Then Derrida goes on: 'And because she does not believe in truth (still, she does find that uninteresting truth in her interest) woman remains a model, only this time a good model.'[55] She has now moved from being a model of truth to a 'good' model of truth. This is my second meaning: it is the denial of all metaphysical claims for 'truth'. Woman does not believe in truth in that sense. So Derrida concludes, 'But because she is a good model, she is in fact a bad model. She plays at dissimulation, at ornamentation, deceit, artifice, at an artist's philosophy. Hers is an affirmative power.'[56] So we arrive at my third meaning of truth: a truth which can and should liberate; it should be an affirmative power. From truth as a recognition of our situation, through to the denial of the possibility of truth, we arrive at the potential our position provides: we can now paint (like an artist) our picture of truth.

As I have argued in Chapters 2 to 4, I think that both Nietzsche and Derrida are entirely mistaken. Although there are mistakes in the details of their argument, the ultimate mistake is in respect to God. I believe that there is a God and the universe is intelligible. However, Nietzsche's great achievement is that he understood what theism entailed. It is not, for Nietzsche, an optional extra on life. He understood completely that God was the safeguard of much that people treat as normal. I concur entirely with Nietzsche that much is at stake once one decides that theism is false. Nietzsche's argument is slightly different from that of Aquinas. Nietzsche moves from the truth about evolution, to the resulting anthropology, to the centrality of psychology, and concludes that therefore rationality is unreliable. Aquinas worked differently: he moved from confidence that the world was intelligible to a quest to justify that intelligibility, and on to the existence of God. However, both share a sense that the effect of God is to protect rationality. In a universe that God intends, then understanding and rationality are intended; in a purposeless universe, understanding and rationality become accidents which might or might not be justified.

The cosy atheism of Russell and others is no longer available. You cannot assume a rationality and argue that there is no foundation to that rationality. Either God and rationality go or God and rationality stay. Either Nietzsche or Aquinas. That is our choice.

Notes

1. For more on this distinction, see the earlier discussion in Chapter 3.
2. I have found Maudemarie Clark's summary of interpretations of Nietzsche, especially as they pertain to truth, very helpful. See Maudemarie Clark, *Nietzsche on Truth and Philosophy*, (Cambridge: Cambridge University Press, 1990), chapter 1.
3. See Walter Kaufmann, *Nietzsche: Philosopher, Psychologist, Antichrist*. 4th edition (Princeton: Princeton University Press, 1974).
4. F. Nietzsche, *Beyond Good and Evil*, translated by R. J. Hollingdale with an introduction by Michael Tanner (Harmondsworth: Penguin, 1990), section 14, p. 44.
5. See my earlier discussion of Rorty in Chapter 3.
6. See Jacques Derrida, *Writing and Differance*, translated by Alan Bass (Chicago: University of Chicago Press, 1978).
7. A good general theological treatment of a whole range of Nietzschean themes is found in Paul Avis, *Faith in the Fires of Criticism* (London: Darton, Longman & Todd, 1995), chapter 4.
8. The possible exception to this is his very early material. See for example the five lectures delivered at Basle University called 'On the Future of our Educational Institutions'.
9. Betrand Russell is a good example of this. Nietzsche's contribution is confined to ethics and secondarily as an historical critic. For Russell see *History of Western Philosophy* (London: George Allen & Unwin, 1946), chapter 25. For a good discussion about the interpretation of Nietzsche, see Peter Poellner's introduction. He rightly shares my sense that his style is part of the message, although does not grasp the extent of this. See Peter Poellner, *Nietzsche and Metaphysics* (Oxford: Clarendon Press, 1995), Introduction.
10. F. Nietzsche, *Ecce Homo*, translated by R. J. Hollingdale, introduction by M. Tanner (Harmondsworth: Penguin, 1992), p. 44.
11. Ibid., p. 18. Nietzsche writes, 'I perceive physiologically – smell – the proximity or . . . the innermost parts, the "entrails", of every soul.'
12. J. Derrida, *Spurs, Nietzsche's Styles* (Chicago and London: University of Chicago Press, 1979), p. 101.
13. Ibid., pp. 101–3. Derrida supplements this 'argument' with additional observations about the potential 'pointlessness' of all of Nietzsche's work. Taking a possible unpublished aphorism

of Nietzsche's, namely, 'I have forgotten my umbrella', Derrida suggests that this might be indicative of Nietzsche's entire work. So, Derrida writes, 'To whatever lengths one might carry a conscientious interpretation, the hypothesis that the totality of Nietzsche's text, in some monstrous way, might well be of the type < I have forgotten my umbrella > cannot be denied. Which is tantamount to saying that there is no < totality to Nietzsche's text > not even a fragmentary or aphoristic one' (ibid., p. 133). I am not persuaded by Derrida's view of communication. Instead I am inclined to the view that Nietzsche is attempting to communicate the uncommunicatable. For some acerbic comments on Derrida see Peter Poellner, *Nietzsche and Metaphysics* (Oxford: Clarendon Press, 1995), pp. 26–8. For an interesting comparison of Derrida, Heidegger, and Nietzsche see Ernst Behler, *Confrontations. Derrida, Heidegger, Nietzsche* (Stanford: Stanford University Press, 1991).

14. F. Nietzsche, *The Gay Science*, Book 3, section 125, p. 181.
15. Maudemarie Clark, *Nietzsche on Truth and Philosophy*, p. 96.
16. Famously Martin Heidegger makes the *Nachlass* his sole source for his very influential interpretation of *Nietzsche*. See Martin Heidegger, *Nietzsche*, translated by David Farrell Krell, Joan Stambaugh, Frank Capuzzi. 4 vols. (San Francisco: Harper & Row, 1979–87). For a general survey see Walter Kaufmann's very good introduction in *Philosophy and Truth*, translated and edited by Daniel Breazeale (New Jersey: Humanities Press, 1979).
17. There has been a proliferation of studies in this area. The most recent are: Richard Schacht, *Nietzsche* (London: Routledge & Kegan Paul, 1983), Maudemarie Clark, *Nietzsche on Truth and Philosophy*, Peter Poellner, *Nietzsche and Metaphysics* and Peter Levine, *Nietzsche and the Modern Crisis of the Humanities* (New York: State University of New York Press, 1995). Poellner and Clark are probably the most substantial; however, Levine is probably closer to my more radical interpretation.
18. 'On Truth and Lies in a Nonmoral Sense' in *Philosophy and Truth*, translated and edited by Daniel Breazeale (New Jersey: Humanities Press, 1979), p. 79.
19. Ibid., p. 80 (my italics).
20. Ibid., p. 82.
21. Ibid., p. 84.
22. Ibid., p. 85.

23. F. Nietzsche, *Human, All Too Human*, translated by R. J. Hollingdale, introduction by Richard Schacht (Cambridge: Cambridge University Press, 1996), section 1, p. 12.

24. Ibid., section 1, p.12.

25. Ibid., section 2, p. 13.

26. Ibid., section 9, p. 15.

27. F. Nietzsche, *Beyond Good and Evil*, section 14, p. 44.

28. F. Nietzsche, *Human, All Too Human*, section 11, p. 16.

29. Ibid., section 18, p. 21.

30. Ibid., section 18, p. 21.

31. Ibid., section 18, p. 22.

32. Ibid., section 32, p. 28.

33. Ibid., section 271, p. 127.

34. So for example, Nietzsche does concede that science partly arose thanks to Christianity. In *The Gay Science*, he writes, 'During the last centuries science has been promoted, partly because it was by means of science that one hoped to understand God's goodness and wisdom best – this was the main motive of the great Englishmen (like Newton) . . .' See *The Gay Science*, translated with commentary by Walter Kaufmann (New York: Vintage Books, 1974), Book 1, section 37, p. 105.

35. F. Nietzsche, *The Gay Science*, Book 2, section 57, p. 121.

36. Ibid., Book 2, section 57, p. 121.

37. Ibid., Book 2, section 58, pp. 121–2.

38. Ibid., Book 3, section 110, p. 170.

39. Ibid., Book 3, section 111, p. 172.

40. F. Nietzsche, *Beyond Good and Evil*, section 17, p. 47.

41. Ibid., section 23, pp. 53–4.

42. F. Nietzsche, *The Gay Science*, Book 5, section 111, p. 172.

43. R. J. Hollingdale in F. Nietzsche, *Thus Spake Zarathustra*, translated with an introduction by R. J. Hollingdale (Harmondsworth: Penguin, 1969), pp. 25–6.

44. F. Nietzsche, *Thus Spake Zarathustra*, Part 1, section 3, p. 43.

45. Ibid., Part 1, section 3, p. 43.

46. Ibid., Part 1, section 3, p. 42.

47. Ibid., Part 1, section 3, p. 103. Nietzsche is very proud of this exhortation from Zarathustra. He quotes it at length in *Ecce Homo*. Perhaps a comment on all of Nietzsche's teaching. See Nietzsche, *Ecce Homo*, pp. 5–6.

48. Commentators on Nietzsche range very widely when it comes to the eternal recurrence. Mircea Eliade in *The Myth of the Eternal Return, or Cosmos and History* translated by W. R. Task (Princeton,

1974) treats it as Nietzsche's way of coping with extreme historicism. Arthur Danto in *Nietzsche as Philosopher* (New York, 1965) believes that Nietzsche meant it literally and works hard to defend the doctrine scientifically. However, as he admits, he does not find the arguments very persuasive. And Peter Levine in his *Nietzsche and the Modern Crisis of the Humanities* (Albany: State University of New York Press, 1995) suggests it should be read 'as presenting both an exoteric myth for the herd, and an esoteric doctrine for those able to bear nihilism' (p. 127). Unlike the above, I find Don Cupitt the most helpful: it is the ultimate test of the affirmation of life, see Don Cupitt, *The Sea of Faith* (London: BBC, 1984). This suggestion has the benefit of simplicity and consistency with the rest of Nietzsche's argument.

49. Nietzsche says in *Ecce Homo*, 'The basic conception of the work, the idea of eternal recurrence, the highest formula of affirmation that can possibly be attained . . .' See F. Nietzsche, *Ecce Homo*, p. 69.

50. F. Nietzsche, *Beyond Good and Evil*, Part 2, section 34, pp. 65–6.

51. Ibid., Part 2, section 43, p. 71.

52. F. Nietzsche, *Twilight of the Idols*, translated by Richard Polt, introduction by Tracy Strong (Indianapolis: Hackett Publishing Co., 1997), pp. 23–4.

53. J. Derrida, *Spurs, Nietzsche's Styles*, p. 51.

54. Ibid., p. 67.

55. Ibid., p. 67.

56. Ibid., p. 67.

CHAPTER 6

The implications

The thesis of this book can be put in two ways: negatively, I am claiming that the only adequate protection against nihilism is belief in God; positively, I am claiming that a *justified rationality* depends on the existence of God. Part of the resistance to this conclusion will come from those who have no grasp of the central significance of the theistic claim. As I have already said, modernity has made God an appendage belief. So it is thought that humanists and Christians can live life agreeing about science and basic moral values, but Christians simply have a need to tag God on to their belief system. But this is a completely wrong way to conceive of religious belief. (I suspect that our modern understanding of the term 'belief' is partly responsible for this mistake.) Both Aquinas and Nietzsche show us that God is a transforming belief, central to how we view everything.

My conclusion is that truth judgements require a theistic framework. All traditions that attempt truth judgements but are not theistic are either incomplete (i.e. have not uncovered their epistemological assumptions), or are radically incoherent. This rationality must not be confused with foundationalism, because there is no sense in which this is 'tradition-transcendent'. Instead I have attempted to locate the 'tradition-constituted' rationality of MacIntyre within a cosmological realism, and as part of the theistic tradition. And this rationality includes all the standard tests for intelligibility: First, coherence is required of our world-perspectives. Any self-contradictory world-perspective cannot be true.[1] Moreover, coherence implies that the world is consistent. Any world-perspective radically inconsistent in its description of human life could be judged as less adequate than those that are more consistent. So a world-perspective that claims to be moral yet racist is less adequate than one that is moral and not racist. Secondly, we shall judge a given world-perspective by its explanatory power. The world-perspective that explains the data in a better way than its competitors is more likely to be true.

So then our age has a straight choice: either the affirmation of God as the ground of all rationality or a collapse into a postmodern denial of 'truth', leaving us with nothing but 'self-constructed' signs. In this concluding chapter, I shall now tease out some of the implications of this argument, under three headings: first, the nature of natural theology; second, the inclusivism of theism; and third, the importance of process (as opposed to content) in Christian ethics.

In the introduction, I noted how unpopular natural theology is amongst contemporary theologians. In the conclusion, I want to make explicit the form of natural theology that I have explicated in this book. Natural theology assumes a certain anthropology and a certain view of creation. On anthropology, it takes the view that our reason cannot be so corrupted by the Fall as to make knowledge of God impossible. Christian theology is committed to the 'Fall' (i.e. for my purposes, humanity has certain egotistical tendencies which thwart our capacity to love). The issue which divides Christians is the extent of that Fall. The Reformers felt that it was so extensive that redemption was an essential prerequisite of any knowledge of God. However, for those in the Catholic tradition, this ignored the 'Imago Dei'. Although we are fallen, this has not totally obliterated the Image. We are both created in the Image of God and, simultaneously, fallen. The capacity to reason is part of the Image. (In this sense, Nietzsche was right to see the modern view of humanity emerging from reductionist science as in conflict with the Christian view. He was also right to see the 'transcendent' element to being human, if true, as the ultimate safeguard of reason.)

A Catholic anthropology has the advantage of making sense of the actual behaviour of humanity. People seem to be capable of both horrendous acts of wickedness and acts of altruism and compassion. The Church is not the exclusive domain of all love and compassion. Indeed often it is the exact opposite: atheists are rarely inclined to be as intolerant and petty as Christians often are. In other words, divine virtue is to be found in humans *qua* humans, not necessarily or specially among the 'redeemed'.

Natural theology is possible because we are made in the Image of God. In addition, natural theology is possible because God has made Godself known in the creation. Naturally such theological reflection is primarily dependent on revelation. Given the ontological status of humanity in respect to God, it is absolutely necessary for disclosure to come from God. In this sense, Karl Barth was entirely right. However, as many have pointed out, God's activity in creation more generally also has the potential to become a disclosure of God to humanity. Though it requires humans to recognize the activity, this is no reason to preclude its possibility. On such a view, 'nature' and 'revelation' merge or overlap.

My argument has been that it takes a creation (i.e. an activity involving decision and purpose) to ensure the intelligibility of the universe which is a strict condition for rational reflection and therefore for truth. Natural theology can take a person only as far as theism: but this should be seen as an achievement not a limitation. Given that the vast majority of traditions are seeking the truth of reality, then it is a vital part of Christian witness to illustrate that this very task is impossible without first assuming the reality of God.

The postmodern objection that natural theology assumes a standard of rationality transcending all traditions is mistaken. Instead, what natural theology entails is the 'inclusiveness' of theism. Talk about 'exclusivism', 'inclusivism', and 'pluralism' has become the discourse which dominates the Christian theology of other religions debate. First used in print by Alan Race,[2] it provides a helpful taxonomy for the debate about the salvific status of those in other religious traditions.

Exclusivists are those who believe that only Christians are saved; inclusivists are those who believe that faithful adherents of a different faith tradition might be 'anonymous Christians'; and pluralists are those who believe that the major world faiths provide equally valid ways to salvation.[3] I am intending to use the terminology and apply it to the broader question: how do you explain disagreement?[4]

The exclusivist is tribal: truth is located exclusively in one tradition and expressed by one symbol system. By tradition, I mean a historical community; by 'symbol system' I mean the propositions contained within the images and symbols of a tradition. Inclusivists believe that certain other traditions are pointing in an imperfect way to their symbol system. While the pluralist believes that one should accept all symbol systems as equally true and valid.

Ultimately, any tradition committed to 'critical realism' will be either exclusivist or inclusivist. It is no coincidence that the equivalent of Karl Rahner's idea of 'anonymous Christians' can be found in all the major world faiths. The Gita claims explicitly that all those following other gods are really discovering Krishna.[5] In Judaism, the Noachide laws are a mechanism for embracing the gentile.[6] And in Islam, Christianity and Judaism are described as 'People of the Book' (i.e. in effect, they have a partial understanding of the demands of monotheism).[7] These are all devices that enable the truth of other traditions to be embraced by the symbol system of a different one.

Inclusivism in this form should not be seen as offensive. The problem in every case is disagreement: we are not all Muslims or whatever. Some account needs to be given of the disagreement. An exclusivist sees the disagreement as a matter of intrinsic error which is deeply incompatible with one's own tradition: the inclusivist sees the disagreement in terms of incompleteness. For those who believe in truth, pluralism is not an option. You cannot be a 'critical realist' about your tradition and simultaneously be a pluralist, because you cannot believe that reality is both best explained in terms of your own symbol system and at the same time believe that all symbol systems are equally true.[8] Therefore given a commitment to truth then the most generous explanation for disagreement will be some form of inclusivism.

Inclusivism is not making a 'tradition-transcendent' claim. It freely admits that other traditions become, at best, a subset of a different tradition. A transcendent rationality is not needed. So then the argument of this study is an inclusivist one. All traditions, which attempt to make sense of the world, are really subsets of theism. The very quest for explanation needs to assume theism. And given the complexity of God's world, theists welcome the range of viewpoints.

This leads to the third implication of the book's argument. The future of Christian ethics lies less with content and more with process.[9] The distinction between content and process cannot be a strict one. However, broadly, 'content' stresses propositions that are justified by the internal Christian narrative; 'process' stresses the means by which truth is discovered.

The problem for Christian ethics today is primarily methodological. How do you do Christian ethics in a pluralistic, multicultural world? One popular solution is to confine Christian ethics to the Church. This is the community committed to living as Christ required us to live. We can draw on the riches of our tradition and formulate our ethical insights which the Church should accept. Of course, one does not expect the rest of the world to accept the ethic and, of course, it does not. Indeed, one sees such acceptance as impossible outside the sphere where life is lived in the light of revelation and by grace.

However, so much of our tradition stresses the contribution that the Church can make to the world. We are called to be 'light in the world' and 'the salt of the earth'. Although content is important, it is not the only insight that the Church has to offer. The argument of this book strongly implies a commitment to conversation committed to the discovery of truth.

It is often assumed that a commitment to the possibility of truth is intrinsically intolerant. It is true that some of the groups most vocal about truth are the most reprehensible. When truth becomes an excuse for exclusion and intolerance, then it can be extremely ugly. Naturally there is no intrinsic reason why a commitment to truth should entail this. Scientists are committed to discovering the truth about the universe and yet no one imagines that this commitment will necessarily result in intolerance. Although the Christian tradition is committed to a God who enables truth to be a possibility, this does not imply that the Christian tradition contains all the truth. If truth in science is difficult to discover, then how much harder is truth in metaphysics? God could have made things clearer, but it seems clear that God desires ambiguity and complexity.

To suggest that God desires ambiguity and complexity will come as a surprise to some. Some Christians talk about a 'simple gospel', where the truth of Christianity is self-evidently true. However, the 'experience' of many (and the education of some) runs counter to this perception of Christianity. In a number of situations most of us find it hard to discover 'what we should do'. Life is rarely black and white, but grey. But the discovery that the truth of God's world is not simple but complex should not be a matter of despair. For the benefits that arise from this complexity suggest strongly that the very difficulties involved in discovering the truth are 'revelatory' about the nature of God and the nature of humanity in community. In short, the benefits are such that the Church should talk about 'complexity' as part of God's world.

What are these benefits? There are, I suggest, three benefits which arise from the ambiguity and complexity of the ethical.[10] First, ethical pluralism (or the term I prefer – ethical plurality) is inevitable. The ambiguity is bound to generate different ethical positions: diversity and disagreement are always going to be with us. In the first instance this is an effect of ambiguity; but I list it as a benefit because I believe diversity is inherently beneficial. Second, this ambiguity inculcates in us the necessity of humility. Although some things are clearer than others, for example the need to protect innocent human life, many things are not so clear. We need to hold our understanding of the truth with humility. And third, this ambiguity encourages conversation and dialogue. We need each other to illuminate the intractable difficulties facing our age. It is in dialogue that truth will be illuminated, contrasts realised, disagreements recognized and of course confronted.

It may even be said that it is for these three reasons that God intended the complexity and ambiguity of the ethical domain. Ethical plurality should be celebrated: diversity and disagreement are part of God's world. The ambiguity is intended because it is God's chosen mechanism to bring about conversation between those who disagree; it is intended precisely because it encourages diversity and disagreement.[11]

The idea that diversity and disagreement are revelatory needs unpacking. At the biblical level the position is not what it may seem. Within the Bible there are passages that resist the notion of human diversity: there is the old story of Babel, seeing variety of languages as a curse inflicted for human hubris, and in the New Testament, some writers are alarmed as cracks in Christian unity make their appearance and diversity of Christian outlook even seems pervasive. However, for all the overt aspiration for uniformity, it is clear that the Bible reflects significant disagreement and diverse positions. Chronicles sits alongside Kings, even though there are clearly different theological outlooks at work. Matthew, Mark, and Luke are all in the canon, even though they clearly disagree. Paul was at variance on certain crucial matters with the Jerusalem apostles. So although we lack explicit reference to justify my desire to celebrate disagreement and though biblical diversity has traditionally been ignored, the actual form of the Bible, critically understood, clearly supports my claim. It is a book that embraces disagreement and diversity, precisely because of the complexity of its subject matter.[12]

Coupled with these reflections on the Bible, I want to argue that diversity and difference must be intended by God because he (or she, because of course God is beyond gender) built it into the creation. The argument needs to be formulated thus: the Christian-Judaeo God is the God of the whole universe. This God is responsible for the Big Bang fifteen billion years ago; it is the God responsible for the vastness of space, the diversity of life-forms, and the emergence of different peoples in different parts of the world. It seems a very attenuated view of the cosmic God to imagine that God is only involved in the history of ancient Israel starting with Abraham and then the Church as it spread through Europe. It is a very impoverished faith which leaves Satan with most of the world and God dabbling in Israel and then Europe. Given that all good things come from God, then God must have been involved when Confucius taught in China. God must have been involved somehow when the Upanishads were being written. God must have not only allowed but delighted in the wisdom of the Buddha.

Yet we feel that all this diversity is confusing, so much so that, as it were, a respectable deity could not be mixed up in it or recognizable through it. We much prefer that God simply provided one clear revelation: Jesus, the apostles, and the Magisterium perhaps, rather than muddy the scene with all these different religions.

That God has not made things simple and clear is manifestly true. Magisteria have always had their work cut out: always adjusted, often belatedly, to circumstances and to new kinds of awareness, while finding ways of denying any such behaviour.

What we need to do is to make dialogue (or a preferable term, 'conversation'; a conversation is wider and more varied than a dialogue) central. To find a way forward, we need each other: we need conversation. Conversation is not an end in itself. We converse for two reasons. First, because we believe that conversation is preferable to conflict. It is the ambiguity and complexity of human situations that often leads to conflict. If conversation is not encouraged, then conflict is often the result. Second, we do so in the hope that conversation will generate new and better options for the way forward. Our goal remains the same – a life of virtue and a just society, where all are able to participate. Inspired by the promise of God's kingdom, we are called to transform the present into what God always intended.

The ultimate safeguard for an authentically liberal Christian tradition is a commitment to truth. Much modern liberalism is built on the foundation of historical relativism.[13] Yet as we saw with John Milbank it is perfectly possible to accept entirely a robust historicism yet, simultaneously, affirm a strongly conservative account of faith.[14] Truth, coupled with an appropriate regard for complexity, entails the need for disagreement, debate, and conversation. Faithfulness to the Christian tradition involves debate and discussion.

Christians should be encouraging all those who believe in 'truth' to converse, that is, to bring our mutual insights and offer our visions of the future to each other. This is not a compromise of the gospel, but rather part of it.

Notes

1. So, for example, a world-perspective that insisted on talking about 'square-circles' would be incoherent. For, as these terms are currently understood, squares are shapes with sides and angles, circles have no sides and no angles, therefore one cannot have a shape with both sides and angles, and yet no sides and no angles.

2. See Alan Race, *Christians and Religious Pluralism* (London: SCM Press, 1983). In the second edition he provides a very interesting defence of pluralism.

3. John Hick in *An Interpretation of Religion* (London: Macmillan, 1989) has provided a very elegant statement of the pluralist hypothesis. For inclusivism, see Gavin D'Costa's *Theology and Religious Pluralism* (Oxford: Blackwell, 1986). For exclusivism, see Harold Netland, *Dissonant Voices* (Leicester: Apollos, 1991). My position on this debate is set out in 'Creating Options: Shattering the Exclusivist, Inclusivist, and Pluralist Paradigm', *New Blackfriars*, 74 (867) (1993): 33–41.

4. The whole issue of 'explaining disagreement' has been a major theme of my work. For those interested see: 'World Perspectives and Arguments: Disagreements about Disagreements', *Heythrop Journal*, 30 (1) (1989): 1–12, and 'Faith and Reason: Reflections on MacIntyre's "Tradition-Constituted Enquiry"', *Religious Studies*, 27 (1991): 259–67. Reprinted in J. Astley and L. J. Francis (eds.), *Critical Perspectives on Christian Education* (Leominster: Gracewing, 1994): 484–93. And my *Plurality and Christian Ethics* (Cambridge: Cambridge University Press, 1994).

5. See *The Bhagavad Gita* (New York: Bantam Books, 1986).

6. I am grateful for many discussions with David Friend on the nature of the Noachide Laws. See his unpublished MA thesis,

The Noachide Covenant in Biblical and Rabbinic Tradition, University of Exeter. See also Helen Fry's reader *Christian–Jewish Dialogue: A Reader* (Exeter: University of Exeter Press, 1996).

7. See *The Koran Interpreted* translated by Arthur Arberry (Oxford: Oxford University Press, 1964).

8. Inclusivism does not entail that one's own symbol system is complete. Of course no religious tradition can claim to have the complete truth about the divine mystery. However, even a partial understanding of the truth about God entails the exclusion of some other views of God; so God is personal rather than non-personal, or good rather than bad. Strictly pluralism does not even allow this because it would mean that Buddhism would be ranked below the theistic traditions. Pluralism, in the end, entails agnosticism.

9. I am extremely grateful to Malcolm Brown's very illuminating use of my work, especially, my *Plurality and Christian Ethics*. For Malcolm Brown see the concluding chapter in *Unemployment and the Future of Work. An Enquiry for the Churches* (CCBI, 1997).

10. I develop this argument in more detail in my professorial inaugural lecture 'Shades of Grey: The Pope, Christian Ethics, and the Ambiguity of Human Situations'. This was reproduced in *Briefing: Official Documentation Service*, 27 (6) (1997): 28–40. In this lecture, I offer the following definitions of complexity and ambiguity: 'By complexity I mean the inter-locking matrix of factors that need to be taken into account when making moral decisions. This leads to ambiguity because our intentions have to take so many conflicting factors into account that we end up with less than satisfactory outcomes.

11. By this, I do not mean that God made things so that life may be a glorified academic seminar. By conversation I mean the creation of relationships with others that can embrace difference and learn from it. It is achievement of such maturity that the very differences between people contribute to the whole.

12. For a more developed form of this argument, see J. L. Houlden, *Bible and Belief* (London: SPCK, 1991), chapter 11.

13. See for example, D. Nineham, *The Use and the Abuse of the Bible* (London: Macmillan, 1976).

14. See Chapter 2.

Bibliography

Anscombe, E., 'Modern moral philosophy', *Philosophy*, 33 (1958).

Alison, H., *Kant's Transcendental Idealism. An Interpretation and Defence* (New Haven: Yale University Press, 1983).

Anselm, *St. Anselm's Proslogion*, translated and edited by M. J. Charlesworth (Oxford: Clarendon Press, 1965).

Anselm, *Anselm of Canterbury*, Volume 1, translated by J. Hopkins and H. Richardson (London: SCM Press, 1974).

Anselm, *Anselm of Canterbury*, Volume 2, translated by J. Hopkins and H. Richardson (Toronto and New York: Edwin Mellen Press, 1976).

Aquinas, Thomas, *Summa Theologiae*, 1a, 2–11, translated by T. McDermott (London: Blackfriars 1964).

Aquinas, Thomas, *Summa Theologiae*, 1a, 19–26, translated by Thomas Gilby (London: Blackfriars 1967).

Aquinas, Thomas, *Summa Theologiae*, 1a, 44–9, translated by Thomas Gilby (London: Blackfriars 1967).

Aquinas, Thomas, *Summa Theologiae*, 2a 2ae, 8–16, translated by Thomas Gilby (London: Blackfriars 1975).

Augustine, *The Problem of Free Choice*, translated by Mark Pontifex (London: Longmans, 1955).

Avis, P., *Faith in the Fires of Criticism* (London: Darton Longman & Todd 1995).

Barr, J., *Biblical Faith and Natural Theology* (Oxford: Clarendon Press, 1993).

Behler, E., *Confrontations. Derrida, Heidegger, Nietzsche* (Stanford: Stanford University Press, 1991).

The Bhagavad Gita (New York: Bantam Books, 1986).

Bradley, F. H., *Essays on Truth and Reality* (Oxford: Clarendon Press, 1914).

Brümmer, V., *Theology and Philosophical Inquiry* (Basingstoke: Macmillan, 1981).

Buckley, M., *At the Origins of Modern Atheism* (New Haven: Yale University Press, 1987).

Byrne, P., *Natural Religion and the Nature of Religion* (London: Routledge, 1989).

Chadwick, H., *Augustine* (Oxford: Oxford University Press, 1986).

Clark, M., *Nietzsche on Truth and Philosophy* (Cambridge: Cambridge University Press, 1990).

Cowdell, S., *Atheist Priest? Don Cupitt and Christianity* (London: SCM Press, 1988).

Craig, W. L., *The Cosmological Argument from Plato to Leibniz* (Basingstoke: Macmillan, 1980).

Craig, W. L. and Smith, Q., *Theism, Atheism, and Big Bang Cosmology* (Oxford: Clarendon Press,1993).

Cupitt, D., *The Sea of Faith* (London: BBC, 1984).

Cupitt, D., *The Long-Legged Fly* (London: SCM Press, 1987).

Cupitt, D., *Creation out of Nothing* (London: SCM Press, 1990).

Danto, A., *Nietzsche as Philosopher* (New York, 1965).

D'Costa, G., *Theology and Religious Pluralism* (Oxford: Blackwell, 1986).

D'Costa, G., (ed.) *Christian Uniqueness Reconsidered: The Myth of a Pluralistic Theology of Religion* (Maryknoll: Orbis Books, 1990).

Derrida, J., *Writing and Differance*, translated by Alan Bass (Chicago: University of Chicago Press, 1978).

Derrida, J., *Spurs, Nietzsche's Styles* (Chicago and London: University of Chicago Press, 1979).

Descartes, *The Philosophical Writings of Descartes* translated by John Cottingham, Robert Stoothoff, and Dugald Murdock II (Cambridge: Cambridge University Press, 1984).

Devitt, M., *Realism and Truth* (Princeton: Princeton University Press, 1984).

Eliade, M., *The Myth of the Eternal Return, or Cosmos and History*, translated by W. R. Task (Princeton, 1974).

Evans, G. R., *Anselm* (London: Geoffrey Chapman, 1989).

Evnine, S., *Donald Davidson* (Stanford: Stanford University Press, 1991).

Flew, A., *David Hume. Philosopher of Moral Science* (Oxford: Basil Blackwell, 1986).

Fowl, S., 'Could Horace Talk with the Hebrews? Translatability and Moral Disagreement in MacIntyre and Stout' in *Journal of Religious Ethics*, 19 (1) (Spring 1991): 1–20.

Friend, D., *The Noachide Covenant in Biblical and Rabbinic Tradition*, unpublished MA thesis, University of Exeter, 1995.

Fry, H., *Christian-Jewish Dialogue: A Reader* (Exeter: University of Exeter Press, 1996).

Gale, R., *On the Nature and Existence of God* (Cambridge: Cambridge University Press, 1991).

Gaskin, J. C. A., *The Quest for Eternity* (Harmondsworth: Penguin, 1984).

Geivett, R. D., *Evil and the Providence of God* (Philadelphia: Temple University Press, 1993).

Gilson, E., *The Christian Philosophy of Saint Augustine*, translated by L. E. M. Lynch (London: Victor Gollancz, 1961).

Haack, S., *Philosophy of Logics* (Cambridge: Cambridge University Press, 1978).

Hebblethwaite, B. L., 'God and Truth', in *Kerygma und Dogma*, 40 (1): 2–18.

Hebblethwaite, B. L., *The Ocean of Truth* (Cambridge: Cambridge University Press, 1988).

Heidegger, M., *Nietzsche*, translated by David Farrell Krell, Joan Stambaugh, Frank Capuzzi. 4 vols. (San Francisco: Harper & Row, 1979–87).

Hick, J., *Faith and Knowledge* (London: Fount, 1957).

Hick, J., *Evil and the God of Love* (London: Collins, 1968).

Hick, J., *The Interpretation of Religion* (Basingstoke: Macmillan, 1989).

Horton, J. and Mendus, S. (eds.), *After MacIntyre* (Cambridge: Polity Press, 1994).

Horwich, P., *Truth* (Oxford: Basil Blackwell, 1990).

Hospers, J., *An Introduction to Philosophical Analysis* (London: Routledge, 1990) 3rd edition.

Houlden, J. L., *Backward into Light* (London: SCM, 1987).

Houlden, J. L., *Bible and Belief* (London: SPCK, 1991).

Hume, D., *Dialogues Concerning Natural Religion* (London: Hafner Press, 1948).

Hume, D., *A Treatise of Human Nature*, edited by L. A. Selby-Bigge (Oxford: Clarendon Press, 1978).

James, W., *Pragmatism: a new name for some old ways of thinking; [and] The meaning of truth: a sequel to 'Pragmatism'* (Cambridge, Mass.: Harvard University Press, 1978).

Jones, G., *Critical Theology* (Cambridge: Polity Press, 1995).

Kant, I., *Logic*, translated by R. Hartman and W. Schwarz (New York: The Bobbs-Merrill Company, 1974).

Kaufmann, W., *Nietzsche: Philosopher, Psychologist, Antichrist.* 4th edition (Princeton: Princeton University Press, 1974).

Kenny, A., *Wittgenstein* (London: Penguin, 1973).

Kolenda, K., *Philosophy Democratised* (Florida: University of South Florida Press, 1990).

The Koran Interpreted, translated by Arthur Arberry (Oxford: Oxford University Press, 1964).

Levine, P., *Nietzsche and the Modern Crisis of the Humanities* (New York: State University of New York Press, 1995).

Lewis, C. and Langford, C., 'The Development of Symbolic Logic' in I. Copi and J. Gould (eds.), *Contemporary Readings in Logical Theory* (New York: Macmillan, 1967).

Loughlin, G., 'Christianity at the end of the story or the return of the master-narrative' in *Modern Theology*, 8 (4) (October 1992): 376–84.

Macdonald, S., 'Aquinas, Thomas' in J. Dancy and E. Sosa (eds.), *A Companion to Epistemology* (Oxford: Basil Blackwell, 1992).

McGuiness, B. and Oliveri, G. (eds.), *The Philosophy of Michael Dummett* (Dordrecht: Kluwer Academic Publishers, 1994).

MacIntyre, A., *A Short History of Ethics* (New York: Macmillan, 1966).

MacIntyre, A., *After Virtue* (London: Duckworth, 1985. 2nd edition).

MacIntyre, A., *Whose Justice? Which Rationality?* (London: Duckworth, 1988).

MacIntyre, A., *Three Rival Versions of Moral Enquiry: Encylopedia, Genealogy and Tradition* (London: Duckworth, 1990).

Markham, I. S., 'Shades of Grey: The Pope, Christian Ethics, and the Ambiguity of Human Situations' in *Briefing: Official Documentation Service*, 27 (6) (1997): 28–40.

Markham, I. S., 'World Perspectives and Arguments: Disagreements about Disagreements' in *Heythrop Journal*, 30 (1) (1989): 1–12.

Markham, I. S., 'Faith and Reason: Reflections on MacIntyre's "tradition-constituted enquiry"' in *Religious Studies*, 27 (1991): 259–67.

Markham, I. S., 'Creating Options: Shattering the "Pluralist, Inclusivist, and Exclusivist" paradigm' in *New Blackfriars*, 74 (1993): 33–41.

Markham, I. S., *Plurality and Christian Ethics* (Cambridge: Cambridge University Press, 1994).

Mascall, E., *Existence and Analogy* (London: Darton, Longman & Todd, 1949).

Mascall, E., *He Who Is: A study in traditional theism* (London: Darton, Longman & Todd, 1966).

Meynell, H., *The Intelligible Universe* (London: Macmillan, 1982).

Milbank, J., *Theology and Social Theory* (Oxford: Basil Blackwell, 1990).

Mitchell, B., *The Justification of Religious Belief* (London: Macmillan Press, 1973).

Moore, G. E., *Some Main Problems in Philosophy* (London: Allen & Unwin, 1953).

Netland, H., *Dissonant Voices* (Leicester: Apollos, 1991).

Newlands, G., *Generosity and the Christian Future* (London: SPCK, 1997).

Nietzsche, F., *Twilight of Idols and the Anti-Christ*, translated by R. J. Hollingdale (Baltimore: Penguin, 1968).

Nietzsche, F., *Thus Spake Zarathustra*, translated with an introduction by R. J. Hollingdale (Harmondsworth: Penguin, 1969).

Nietzsche, F., *The Gay Science*, translated by Walter Kaufmann (New York: Vintage Books, 1974).

Nietzsche, F., *Philosophy and Truth*, translated and edited by Daniel Breazeale (New Jersey: Humanities Press, 1979).

Nietzsche, F., *Beyond Good and Evil*, translated by R. J. Hollingdale with an introduction by Michael Tanner, (Harmondsworth: Penguin, 1990).

Nietzsche, F., *Ecce Homo*, translated by R. J. Hollingdale, introduction by M. Tanner (Harmondsworth: Penguin, 1992).

Nietzsche, F., *Human All Too Human*, translated by R. J. Hollingdale, introduction by Richard Schacht (Cambridge: Cambridge University Press, 1996).

Nineham, D., *The Use and the Abuse of the Bible* (London: Macmillan, 1976).

O'Hagan, T., 'Searching for Ancestors' in *Radical Philosophy*, 54 (2) (1990): 19–22.

Phillips, D. Z., *Faith after Foundationalism* (London: Routledge, 1988).

Phillips, D. Z., *Belief, Change and Forms of Life* (Basingstoke: Macmillan, 1986).

Plato, *Sophist*, translated by Nicholas White (Indianapolis: Hackett Publishing Co., 1993).

Poellner, P., *Nietzsche and Metaphysics* (Oxford: Clarendon Press, 1995).

Polkinghorne, J., *Science and Christian Belief* (London: SPCK, 1994).

Popper, K., 'A Realist View of Logic, Physics, and History', in W. Yourgrau and A. Breck (eds.), *Physics, Logic and History* (New York/London: Plenum Press, 1970).

Putnam, H., 'Three-Valued Logic' in *Philosophical Studies*, 8 (5) (October 1957): 73–80.

Quine, W. V. O., *Word and Object* (Cambridge, Mass: MIT Press, 1960).

Race, A., *Christians and Religious Pluralism* (London: SCM Press, 1983).

Ramsey, I.T., *Religious Language* (London: SCM Press, 1957).

Rorty, R., *Philosophy and the Mirror of Nature* (Oxford: Basil Blackwell, 1980).

Rorty, R., *Consequences of Pragmatism* (Minnesota: Minnesota University Press, 1982).

Russell, B., *Mysticism and Logic* (London: Longmans, 1919).

Russell, B., *History of Western Philosophy* (London: George Allen & Unwin, 1946).

Russell, B., *Why I Am Not a Christian* (London: Unwin, 1967).

Schacht, R., *Nietzsche* (London: Routledge & Kegan Paul, 1983).

Southern, R. W., *Saint Anselm: A Portrait in a Landscape* (Cambridge: Cambridge University Press, 1990).

Swinburne, R., *The Coherence of Theism* (Oxford: Clarendon Press, 1977).

Swinburne, R., *The Existence of God* (Oxford: Clarendon Press, 1979).

Swinburne, R., *Faith and Reason* (Oxford: Clarendon Press, 1981).

Taylor, C., *Sources of the Self* (Cambridge: Harvard University Press, 1989).

Trigg, R., *Reason and Commitment* (Cambridge: Cambridge University Press, 1973).

Trigg, R., *Reality at Risk. A Defence of Realism in Philosophy and the Sciences* (New York: Harvester Wheatsheaf, 1989).

Unemployment and the Future of Work. An Enquiry for the Churches (CCBI, 1997).

Ward, K., *Holding Fast To God* (London: SPCK, 1982).

Ward, K., *Rational Theology and the Creativity of God* (Oxford: Basil Blackwell, 1982).

Ward, K., *Images of Eternity* (London: Darton, Longman & Todd, 1987).

Wilson, B. (ed.), *Rationality* (Oxford: Basil Blackwell, 1970).

Winch, P., *The Idea of a Social Science* (London: Routledge & Kegan Paul, 1958).

Index of Authors

Index of Subjects